Don't Go to College

"Don't let schooling interfere with your education."
—**Mark Twain**

DON'T GO TO
College
A Case for Revolution

Michael J. Robillard   **Timothy J. Gordon**
M.A., M.A., Ph.D.   M.A., Ph.L., J.D.

Foreword by
Michael Knowles, B.A., Yale

Afterword by
John Henry Cardinal Newman, B.A., D.D.

Regnery Publishing
WASHINGTON, D.C.

Regnery® is a registered trademark and its colophon is a trademark of Salem Communications Holding Corporation

Cataloging-in-Publication data on file with the Library of Congress

ISBN: 978-1-68451-297-3
eISBN: 978-1-68451-312-3

Library of Congress Control Number: 2022937289

Published in the United States by
Regnery Publishing,
A Division of Salem Media Group
Washington, D.C.
www.Regnery.com

Manufactured in the United States of America

10 9 8 7 6 5 4 3 2 1

Books are available in quantity for promotional or premium use. For information on discounts and terms, please visit our website: www.Regnery.com.

CONTENTS

FOREWORD

The most memorable scene on the Bayeux Tapestry depicts a man smacking another man with a large stick beneath the caption "Here Bishop Odo, holding a club, comforts the boys." Odo's vocation precluded him from actual fighting at the Battle of Hastings. But the bishop was permitted to help rally the troops for his half brother William, who conquered England in 1066. This tough concept of comfort tends to shock modern sensibilities accustomed to "safe spaces." Fortunately for the Normans, Odo was an eleventh-century prelate rather than a twenty-first-century academic, so he understood that to comfort means to give strength. Odo did not intend to hurt the boys; on the contrary, he wanted to encourage them to get back onto the battlefield. Bishop Odo smacked because he loved.

In *Don't Go To College*, Michael Robillard and Tim Gordon smack the university because they love the university, where they have spent much of their lives earning eight degrees between them. Unfortunately, universities no longer arm their charges for the intellectual, political, and spiritual battles that they will face upon graduation. Or rather, they do not arm them in such a way as to help them win the fight of their lives over ignorance, decay, and damnation.

Many contemporary critics of higher education contend that a college degree no longer means anything. But as Robillard and Gordon show, that fêted credential still means quite a lot—and none of it good. Today a college degree implies stunted maturity, philosophical incoherence, crippling debt, and at least a species or two of venereal disease.

Liberal education exists to train students in the subjects and skills necessary to make them free people. No less important than the seven liberal arts—grammar, logic, rhetoric, arithmetic, astronomy, music, and geometry—are the seven virtues: faith, hope, charity, justice, temperance, prudence, and fortitude. Liberal education cultivates not merely the mind but also the will to tame the student's appetites and strengthen his rational will. Both ignorance and vice compromise a man's freedom; a proper education must address the whole man.

Today, institutions that purport to offer a liberal education usually deliver the opposite. Professors peddle fashionable lies and obscure eternal truths. Administrators mock virtue and subsidize vice. The whole experience often leaves students less educated than they were when they matriculated. In 2007, the Intercollegiate Studies Institute administered a sixty-question quiz on American history and civics to twenty-eight thousand freshmen and seniors at more than eighty college and universities around the United States. At most schools, the seniors fared no better than the freshmen; at many schools, they performed worse.

Even a cursory look at the history of the American university reveals just how far our system of higher education has fallen. From America's earliest colonial days into the nineteenth century, university commencement ceremonies entailed graduates giving orations in Latin, Greek, and Hebrew, as well as formal "disputations" on philosophical questions. In the 1650s, Harvard might have denied a student his degree if he could not explain how "form is the principle of individuation" or why "the soul does not come into existence from the physical contribution of the parents." As late as 1810, a Harvard man had to explain at commencement why "God demands the actions which beget happiness" and "prohibits those which bring misery" to obtain his degree. In 2003, the commencement festivities at America's most prestigious university demanded nothing more of the graduating class than that they show up and listen to Will Ferrell recount his favorite sketches from *Saturday Night Live.*

Comedians have become regular fixtures at commencement ceremonies in recent years: Maya Rudolph at Tulane, Jon Stewart at William and Mary, Stephen Colbert at the University of Virginia, Conan O'Brien at Dartmouth. The list goes on. Comedy routines are routinely the capstones of a college career because higher education is now a farce, and benighted graduates are the unwitting butts of the joke.

One doubts that most college students today have ever heard of Bishop Odo or even the Battle of Hastings, so thoroughly have radical ideologues conquered the university and perverted curricula to their own destructive ends. But the fight for truth rages on. In *Don't Go to College*, Robillard and Gordon offer urgent comfort to those seekers of wisdom willing to endure the tough love of a true education.

Michael Knowles
Nashville, Tennessee
May 9, 2022

CHAPTER ONE

Why Go to College?

*"Have the courage to have your wisdom
regarded as stupidity."*

—Antonin Scalia

The average American college hopeful would be better off drilling a hole in his head than attending a present-day university. He'd learn about as much, wouldn't be financially crippled with student debt, and would likely avoid acquiring a variety of sexually transmitted diseases. And if a drill to the head sounds like self-harm, what do you think four to six years of safe spaces, trigger warnings, grievance studies, and neo-Marxist indoctrination amounts to, if not an expensively acquired ritual lobotomy?

Most people today go to college not for a deep, decades-long dive into ancient languages or philosophy, but rather for the prosaic reasons given by the character Jack Gaines in the movie *Accepted*: "Society has rules. And the first rule is: You go to college. You want to have a happy and successful life? You go to college. If you want to be somebody, you go to college. If you want to fit in, you go to college."[1]

Today, though, if you're facing facts, college has become a *detriment* to a happy, successful life, given the years and money you will waste on courses that you will never need and that will only help you "fit in" if by "fitting in" you mean becoming a "politically correct" mantra-drone. (What is "correct" in this sense is factually, scientifically, and philosophically wrong.)

Needless to say, that's not what college was supposed to be—but that's what it is, at least in about 99 percent of the nation's colleges and universities. The university, as an institution, was founded in the Middle Ages. Its purpose was to teach Christian Aristotelianism. American universities were founded in much the same spirit, but also to create civic-minded, moral citizens. One might even go so far as to say the modern-day American university has *completely inverted* what the medieval university and America's founding universities set out to achieve. Instead, America's universities now function as institutional, "skills-based" assembly lines to produce citizen-serfs for the global economy, tutored in an ideology of obedience to Big LGBTQ+, Big Tech, Big Government, Big Media, Big Business, the Big Nonprofits, and of course Big Education—the latter of which confers the credentialing keys to the kingdom. How often do we hear parents say that their sons and daughters were conservative, Christian, happy, independent thinkers *before* going to college, only to emerge on the other side brainwashed and woke, faithless and unhappy, underemployed and broke.

If that's the result, why go—why send our kids—to college? Don't go! Under Jack Gaines's foolish yet understandable misapprehension, college remains a universal cultural goal so long as it guarantees social and financial success: if a college education will make me rich, then I'll put up with whatever tomfoolery the academicians put me through. That "if-then" statement is still reiterated throughout our culture. Even when, as in our day, this statement has not proven to be true, most students and parents don't blame the college or university; they blame *not majoring in the right subject*, or *not studying hard enough*, or *not having done enough internships*. They don't blame the rapacious institution itself for inflicting massive student debt, requiring noxious rather than edifying courses, and encouraging students to waste years in immoral idleness and destabilizing indoctrination. But they should hold the colleges accountable.

A big part of the problem is the refusal of students, parents, and the alleged guardians of American culture—*conservatives*—to truly acknowledge just how bad things are in our universities. The criticisms you generally hear about political bias on campus, the refusal to allow conservative speakers a forum, and crazy professors saying crazy things, are usually written off as "kids will be kids" and "professors will be liberal."

But it's so much worse than that, almost unbelievably so. As the British journalist (and Oxford graduate) James Delingpole has written: "Universities are madrassas for woke stupidity."[2] It is long past time for a *revolutionary* reconsideration of—and largescale student withdrawal from—our colleges and universities. In 1951, William F. Buckley Jr. warned Americans—especially concerned college alumni—of the need to restore traditional standards to our colleges in his classic book *God and Man at Yale*.[3] Today, three-quarters of a century later, the situation has immeasurably degraded. Four generations of Americans have filtered haplessly through universities like lambs to the slaughter, the chief purpose of which has been to germinate within them ideas so potently subversive as to undermine their belief in Christianity, in objective morality itself, in their country, and in traditional American norms. With each succeeding generation, the effort has become more blatant, more extreme, and has been conducted with fewer restraints. In consequence, what we need now is not reform, but revolution.

Aristotle tells us in the fifth book of the *Politics* that men begin revolutions on account of their private lives, thus the reader has every right to ask who we might be, the overeducated authors of this treatise against modern higher education. So please indulge us with a lengthier-than-normal introduction of ourselves. We come at this as Christian reverts trained in philosophy, cured with real-world experience from our youths; as itinerant philosophers abroad; as reformed, world-weary fools who, like Saint Augustine, found truth at last at our starting point—that is, in our own spurned faith; as signs of contradiction inside the academy, one as a stoic infantry officer and the other as a brawling nightclub rocker.

Michael Robillard

I grew up in a small, blue-collar suburb just south of Boston in the 1980s. My father was a warehouseman—a strong, silent, stoic type. To date, the he is the hardest working man I've ever met. My mother was a traditional housewife. To date, she is the kindest soul I've ever met. It was a loving, traditional, Irish Catholic family that included a younger sister.

In retrospect, it was a wonderful childhood. Like Frodo's experience growing up in the Shire, my childhood existence was exceptionally wholesome, innocent, and, admittedly, quite sheltered. Family and grandparents, aunts and uncles, church on Sunday, Little League in the spring, pets, trips to the New Hampshire wilderness in the summer, Christmas and Easter gatherings, and Fourth of July cookouts were the norm. G. I. Joe, *Super Mario Bros.*, and *Star Wars* made up the cultural DNA of my youth. So too did long summer nights of sleepovers with cousins, debating whether professional wrestling was "real," riding bikes without helmets at ludicrous speeds, and trying to mimic Michael Jackson's "moonwalk" in socks on the linoleum kitchen floor. On our primitive color television in the living room, I had occasional glimpses of the social and political backdrop of the 1980s Cold War, President Ronald Reagan, Prime Minister Margaret Thatcher, and Pope John Paul II.

In school, I was the typical introverted-bookworm, honor-roll student. I never once skipped school—something that to this day I regret. I was also relatively short and small compared to the other boys my age. I was likewise left-handed, somewhat klutzy, and lacking in hand-eye coordination. In high school, however, I discovered the sport of wrestling, a sport that had weight classes and rewarded raw will, aggression, and analytical thinking (psyching out an opponent, and finding angles of attack). Sometimes in wrestling who won on the mat simply came down to who wanted it more. I greatly appreciated its individual, martial, primal, Spartan spirit.

Aside from wrestling, though, my suburban-Massachusetts public education was anything but manly. Classes were co-ed, teachers predominantly women, and shop class had been mostly phased out for computers. Our reference points were those of the suburb or the city. Not a single kid I knew had a father who made a living as a farmer or a rancher or a dairyman or a fisherman. Likewise, almost none of us hunted, fished, camped, worked on cars, or built things. For most kids, sports were a proxy for religion and culture, and within our classrooms John F. Kennedy and Martin Luther King Jr. were pretty much regarded as secular gods.

Somewhere around my sophomore year of high school, I went to my guidance counselor and told her I wanted to be a veterinarian. Her response was not what I expected. "You know veterinarian schooling is quite expensive, right? How are you going to pay for that? How are your parents going to pay for that? What do your parents do for a living? You have a younger sister, right? Isn't she planning to go to college as well?"

She then gave me a twenty-minute pitch on the military-service academies and how they could provide a top-tier, Ivy League–level education for "free" for a smart, ambitious, blue-collar kid like myself. The only catch was that it required five years of military service upon graduation. It sounded like a challenge. I didn't mind testing myself. And I was proud of my family's military service in World War II and Vietnam. The application process for entry into West Point is long and hard, but in the winter of my senior year, I got accepted. I was West Point bound. In my senior high-school yearbook, I wrote that my life's ambition was "to live a life of honor and virtue." I believed it and meant it.

I began my first year at West Point thinking of myself as a devout Catholic—but my definition of "devout" was, in retrospect, very weak and watered down. A combination of feeble catechesis and a Massachusetts public-school education will do that. Even in the corridors of West Point—a tradition-minded school—I found my Catholic faith unraveling. The Bible-study group I attended seemed more like a group poetry-reading section than something that was theologically satisfying, and I eventually started skipping it in favor of attending a philosophy club. Here, we seemed to discuss the real, deep questions about God, existence, reality, morality, the human condition, and even thinking about *thinking itself*. I wanted more.

Some of this was healthy, some of it was not. It is easy as a young student to be overly impressed by an analytically trained philosopher mopping the floor with callow Christian students unaware of analytical philosophy—and I certainly was. I soon changed my major from military history to philosophy, and my Catholic faith began to crumble, in a stereotypical way. As Catholic philosopher Ed Feser notes:

It's a common story where you start to study philosophy— and especially if you are coming from a religious point

of view, or at least a point of view that takes the existence of God and other religious ideas for granted—and
then you encounter skeptical writers like Nietzsche, or
David Hume, or Bertrand Russell, or someone like that,
you're very impressed by that because you hadn't heard
it before.[4]

That was pretty much my story too. Accordingly, during this
period of my life, I found all these philosophical questions existentially
devastating, and I stared into an abyss wondering if the atheist-
materialists were right. What if God, beauty, truth, the soul, the mind,
and free will were all an illusion? What then? I was surprised that
these questions didn't bother most of my cadet peers, who divided
largely into two camps—Protestant Bible-thumpers or Randian nihil-
ists who would say, "Bro, you think too much. You just need to get
drunk and get laid."

Where my Christian faith used to be, I cobbled together an
ersatz religion of "rights and duties" and not being racist. If I no
longer had God, I still had my country. And in the second week of
my senior year at West Point, on September 11, 2001, my country
got attacked. Overnight, hypothetical classroom discussions
became matters of urgent reality. The subsequent year and a half
was a blur of frenzied activity: classes, talk of deployments to
Afghanistan, graduation, commissioning, checking in to Fort
Benning, Airborne School, Infantry School, freezing misery in
Ranger School, reporting to Fort Bragg—and then our unit was
somehow in Baghdad, Iraq. If I doubted religion before, I thought
of it as something thoroughly corrupt now. It was *religion* that
inspired fanatical jihadists to fly airplanes into buildings full of
innocent civilians. It was *religion*—some sort of evangelical nonsense about spreading democracy and prosperity—that had me

invading the house of an Iraqi family at 3:00 a.m. It was *religion* that covered up the abuses of the Boston Catholic Archdiocese where I grew up.

Returning home, the anti–Iraq War, anti-Bush, and pro-left/ pro-liberal ethos seemed universal, and I fell right into it. Sam Harris, Richard Dawkins, and "The New Atheists" were everywhere to buttress my critique of religion. And just as I had fully lost my religious faith somewhere in the streets of Baghdad, I also lost a large amount of faith in my country and its political leadership. *Every* woman I met coming home seemed to be on the Left. I assumed I had to be too because my politics boiled down to two ideas: racism was wrong and economic inequality was wrong, though these two ideas were held rather vaguely as simply unquestionable truths.

I did know, however, that I didn't have the stomach or desire for a twenty-year career in the military. I knew I was decent at philosophy as an undergrad and that I had a natural thirst for philosophical inquiry. Maybe I could jettison my career as an Army officer and try my hand at being a philosophy professor instead.

The beginning few years of my time in grad school were a combination of exhilaration, possibility, and, most of all, vindication. Unlike my time in the stifling, hyper-conformist atmosphere of the military, now I was finally home, around *my* people—people who were thoughtful, open-minded, knowledgeable, worldly, lovers of ideas, and appreciators of the life of the mind. No longer the odd-duck soldier who thought too much, I felt, for the very first time in my adult life, like I was finally accepted.

For the most part, many of my professors and my graduate peers found me to be somewhat of a refreshing anomaly, coming from a background quite different from theirs. I was the thoughtful, philosophical soldier, critical of our country's recent wars. During that time period, I could also sleep easily at night with a clear conscience knowing I was now one of "the good people." I thought of myself—and my colleagues—as liberal and tolerant. Our opponents were the reverse.

I finished my Ph.D. at the University of Connecticut and then secured a slot in a four-year post-doctoral program at the University of Oxford, starting in 2017. I thought I had finally achieved my life's goal. But while I was at Oxford, I recognized something that I had only vaguely started suspecting, and tried to ignore, in my dream of pursuing analytical philosophy as a career. The left-liberal philosophers that I thought of as cool, calm, and dispassionate were really, in fact, nothing of the sort. That was, at best, a pose they adopted when they faced students. But, under pressure, they cracked.

The twin shocks in 2016 of Donald Trump's presidential victory in the United States and British voters deciding in favor of Brexit shattered that pose, and I saw left-liberal philosophers turning into hysterical, convulsive, whining conspiracy theorists, grasping at one ad hominem argument after another. These were people who thought that history was inevitably trending their way. Trump and Brexit were the first real losses they had faced since the elections of Ronald Reagan and Margaret Thatcher. The administrations of George W. Bush and of British prime ministers John Major, David Cameron, and Theresa May represented only relatively minor dissent from a greater liberal consensus about globalism and big government.

I was stunned to see my fellow liberals so unhinged, so unbalanced, and so lacking in courage. They appeared incapable of recognizing *any* enemies on their left—especially not from the sudden onrush of the transgender mob and the anti–free speech activists before whom they buckled and capitulated, and even fearfully endorsed. I saw philosophical discussion being shut down at *Oxford University*, an alleged home of free speech, which would have seemed nearly unthinkable to me just a year before.

When I suggested the idea of giving a public philosophy talk on whether a man could *become* a woman by simply claiming to be one, my colleagues strongly discouraged me from doing so on account of the potential loss of donors and funding such a talk might generate, as well as the hiring of security that such a talk would require. Several months later, a colleague of mine, with whom I used to joke about "pronoun madness," now told me that I could expect no more invitations to philosophy conferences if I "went out of my way" to intentionally "misgender" people. I was speechless.

In my idealism, I had assumed that we were committed to truth, reason, and open, rational inquiry. I now discovered that this was a lie. Analytic philosophy as an academic specialty was full of craven careerists and de facto Marxists. The Marxists called the shots, and the liberals conformed. The universities in which we liberal academics worked were, in fact, progressive indoctrination centers. I had missed all this because, as a liberal, I had been one of them. I had transgressed no boundaries. Once I did, I realized that *every conservative* critique of higher education—which I had previously ignored—was utterly true.

I had to retrace my steps. I had come to think of myself as a liberal because I believed in tolerance, open-mindedness, and free, rational inquiry. I came to see that not only did the Left not believe in these things, but that the Left had no sense of perspective. For them, color blindness was racism; caring for others meant erasing national borders; sympathy for people with same-sex attractions necessarily meant accepting an infinite number of "genders"—and these extreme, even nonsensical positions would be aggressively policed, with no allowance for dissent whatsoever.

I realized I needed to rethink all of my starting points, assumptions, and first principles. That led me back to Catholic philosophers like Thomas Aquinas, whom I had so casually dismissed when I saw philosophy as an alternative to theology. With age and experience, these Catholic philosophers seemed wiser, sounder, and more sensible than I had originally thought.

In retrospect, I know that I likely could have stayed and lived very comfortably at Oxford for the rest of my life had I wanted to, keeping my mouth shut, bowing my head, acknowledging the preferred pronouns, and chasing various academic grants and funding streams. But I didn't want to do that. I couldn't live a lie.

I quit my dream position at Oxford in late 2019. I moved back home and began putting my life and fractured worldview back together at age thirty-nine. I went back to church and started writing a public letter about academia that I didn't release for another year. I didn't release it right away because an old colleague of mine contacted me and alerted me to a new post-doctoral position at Notre Dame. I applied and was accepted. I anticipated a better academic climate than I had experienced at Oxford, but to my dismay it was just more of the same, only with COVID-19 masks and pandemic hysteria. I finished my time at Notre Dame in spring of 2021, and this time I left academia for good. In June 2021, I published an essay on Substack titled, "How I Left Academia, or, How Academia Left Me," where it fast gained more than twenty-thousand views. I realized I had struck a chord. (It is reproduced as an appendix to this book.)

I also came across a guy on YouTube, a Catholic scholar and influencer who apparently had been fired from his job at a Catholic school for calling the radical Marxist group Black Lives Matter "a terrorist organization" on Twitter. He immediately won my attention and my respect for telling the truth—no matter the consequences. He was brimming with what Aristotle referred to as *thumos* or "fire in the belly." He offered an intellectual defense of Catholicism and conservatism that was both deeply philosophical and profoundly worldly. And his every criticism of higher education—in which he too had spent his life—was exactly right. He became my coauthor on this book and my ally in seeking a revolution (or counterrevolution) in higher education.

Timothy Gordon

Michael and I are separated by less than a year in age, but whereas he grew up in Boston Celtics country in New England, I grew up in Showtime Laker–era Southern California (with a few stints in North Texas on account of my dad's work in the petroleum industry). Accordingly, his characterization of the post-moral milieu of the 1980s and especially the 1990s goes for my childhood experience as well, notwithstanding his contrasting setting in Celtics country. Coming up through Catholic schools, I did very well academically, won good conduct awards, and was a budding basketball star. Like Holden Caulfield, protagonist of *The Catcher in the Rye*, I was also something of a wise-ass, unafraid—and indeed proud—to express moral exasperation with my libertine peers. Not that I believed the faith any better than they did: literally none of us took seriously the watered down, paper-thin rites of the post–Vatican II Catholic faith being peddled to us—who could? But even in my unbelieving youth, I always loved the Church's natural-law moral philosophy. I did so without the aid of my teachers or priests (who covered up the Church's doctrinal gems in worldly, postconciliar embarrassment). Still, I always loved and even fought for the natural virtues, even if in those days I couldn't tell you why.

My college-prep high school had a risible "honor code." It was supposed to be strictly enforced, but wasn't, and I intuited that the Catholic education I was receiving was a pitifully lame version of the real thing. But in those days, I failed to look any closer at what "the real thing" was. I was being prepared for an agnostic, secular, shallow, unheroic, suburban life—and all along I wanted anything but that. Also, I wasn't seeing eye to eye with my basketball coaches.

Disillusioned, I quit basketball and changed schools for "senior high," namely eleventh and twelfth grades. For the first time in my life, I attended public school, and in place of basketball, I turned to playing live music with a rock band. I got physically bigger, still played lots of basketball (but now it was in my off time), and began getting into fights with and trolling those I deemed "party-scene scumbags," "frauds," or as my secular, adolescent, literary hero Holden Caulfield would have said, "phonies."

After high school, I stayed in Dallas for a scholarship at a local university because my rock band had been landing bigger and bigger gigs, local radio time, and even regional tours. As a college freshman, I was a full-time student and a full-time rocker. I fit in just enough weekly study to make decent grades—which wasn't much study at all, often crammed in before or after gigs—while practicing music and "playing out" at the local nightclub scene as many nights of the week as we could schedule. This involved late hours, dingy nightclubs, occasional street scrums (a carryover from high school), and returning home at 3:30 a.m. even on school nights in garments that reeked of stale smoke. Once when I was on stage, just before delivering a live set, a female classmate had to remind me that we had a chemistry exam the next morning (which I had apparently overlooked on my course syllabus). I got the last-minute studying done in the middle of the night, which fairly characterizes those years of study.

Generally speaking, I had the stamina to live those crazy hours, though on another occasion I fell asleep while writing my Native American History final exam. (This was one of my compulsory courses in the curriculum of "what is institutionally wrong with Western civilization and especially with white people"—my response to it would go from sleeping, literally, to waking up and fighting it.)

Still, not to brag, I was exceedingly good at schooling and especially at hyper-efficiency in paper and exam preparation. This was
particularly true when I was taking classes I cared about (certainly
not Native American History). Between sleepy dawns and raucous
dusks, I got the academic workload done.

More than that, I found my academic passion: philosophy.
Namely, I found it in the figure of Dr. Charles Bambach, a charis-
matic, Jesuit-educated New Yorker who taught me German philosophy. From there, I started down the lengthy footpath back to Rome
via Thomas Aquinas and Aristotle, the two most important thinkers
in the history of Western civilization. I also rekindled an interest in
Russian literature, especially Dostoevsky.

I cut, I suppose, something of a counterintuitive figure. Although
I routinely stumbled into my morning classes bleary-eyed, in smoky-
smelling hoodies, I never once tried marijuana or even a cigarette.
Although I sang in a popular local band, with plenty of female fans
and feminine attention around, I kept rather closely to the virtue of
chastity. Although I engaged in boyish mischief, I was never interested in mindless mayhem; and when I traipsed into classrooms with
occasional black eyes or bruised knuckles from periodic street fights,
they came from fights *against* frat thugs who stumbled, drunk and
looking for trouble (and finding it), around Deep Ellum, the live
music center of Dallas. I never even drank alcohol until after the
band broke up, later in college. I include all these moral details from
my otherwise misspent youth in order to enrich the reader's understanding of the importance, and even unlikeliness, of my reversion
to Christian Aristotelianism. Like all decent young men, I was naturally attracted to morality, and my devotion deepened when I learned
that the philosophical ideas behind Christian morality are 100
percent true. This is the role of *true education*, which, in my case,
was found in part on the providential sidetrack of performing in a

paradoxically clean-living rock band. (Playing our sets perfectly sober had given my band an advantage over other local metal- and hardcore-rock acts, who spurned sobriety; we were more reliable, and therefore more successful.)

The aggressive, "straightedge" music we played in clubs and bigger venues made us counterculture infiltrators—deep-cover training for what I would take up later in life. We might have *looked* a bit like the rockers seen on MTV's *Headbanger's Ball*—well, a tougher "hardcore" version, guys with buzzed hair instead of ponytails—who followed the countervailing credo of the godfather of "straightedge," Ian MacKaye, to not drink, smoke, or screw around. We liked to think of ourselves as both book-smart and street-smart, cool but chaste, tough while naturally virtuous, wild in some ways and yet a paragon of temperance in others. I felt, I confess, morally excellent simply for beating out the anti-Christian cultural curve. What I didn't appreciate then was that repudiating the world's values is a necessary, but not a sufficient, condition for human thriving. I failed to realize what a low bar it was and how much more work there was to do.

Make no mistake: all this has everything to do with education. In graduate school while working on a master's degree in philosophy, at a (nominally) Catholic school for the first time since the tenth grade, I realized that the answers to human thriving were to be found in the plenitude of the Aristotelian intellectual tradition. There was infinitely more depth and utility and truth to the Catholic tradition than in the secular French, German, modern, and postmodern philosophies that had dominated my undergraduate coursework.

After completing my master's degree, I grew intent on making a careful study of Aristotle and Saint Thomas Aquinas. So, my wife and I (we had gotten married young, in between two of my graduate degrees in philosophy) relocated to Rome, Italy, to study under Father Kevin Flannery, one of the world's leading Thomists at the world's oldest Jesuit university, founded by Saint Ignatius of Loyola himself: the Pontifical Gregorian University. It was a veritable charmed life of marital bliss, intellectual discovery, and renewed faith. We took a small, comfy two-bedroom flat in the city's easterly neighborhood of San Lorenzo—within the square mile formed by fully four of the seven basilicas of the See of Rome: our neighborhood's namesake San Lorenzo to the east; Santa Croce in Gerusalemme to the southwest; San Giovanni in Laterano to the northwest; and Santa Maria Maggiore to the north. I passed the Colosseum every day on my way to the Greg (as we called the Gregorian University). My young wife and I bashed around the Eternal City, teaching English part-time together as I worked my way toward a licentiate degree at the old school (and I hoped, an eventual doctorate).

We discovered hidden gems all around the northern and eastern parts of the city: for example, the Capuchin Crypt in Barberini Piazza, made entirely of the remains of Capuchin monks. We attended the opera. We swam and sunbathed at the beaches of Ostia. We ate gelato, purchased pizza by the ounce at Metro windows, and trained for the *Maratona di Roma* together. At home, my wife prepared a manifold of pasta recipes, and we ate it once and sometimes twice a day like Romans. Denizens from five of the seven continents supped at our table, where we enjoyed wine and philosophy. Without a roommate (except for my wife, of course), I became host, and my flat the *locus in quo*, for graduate reading groups in Aristotle, Augustine, and Aquinas. Aside from my new American friend Andrew, such philosophy grad students were mostly priests from all around the world. Andrew regaled us with stories about his idiosyncratic Italian roommate and his hateful pet parrot Eddie, with whom Andrew apparently squabbled incessantly. We showed a pair of Germans Thanksgiving dinner. Literally from the street, we took in a tearful Mormon painter from Utah, who had lost her wallet. She lived with us for a couple weeks, after which she moved to Florence, where we would visit her occasionally.

It was a time of nonstop tourism and an utterly serious study of Thomistic philosophy. My time at the Greg was the wholesomest, jolliest, best-balanced, most-focused, and most-uplifting spiritual, intellectual, and moral "learning experience" I could ever imagine. It was what a real college education should be—*but almost never is, in our culture*—and it was combined with the urgent facts of life.

In November, we learned my wife was pregnant. Abigail was born that summer, one month early, and with an unexplained in utero post-hemorrhagic brain injury. We remained in Rome for most of the autumn, as I turned in my thesis and completed the oral comprehensive exam and the degree. But any plans I had of continuing on for a doctorate were over.

We returned to Los Angeles a week before Thanksgiving in 2008. Like Edmond Dantès, I set foot on a once familiar shore, years later as a foreigner in my own homeplace, with a forever-altered view of it. My plan now became to attend law school in the fall with the hope of supporting my family as a lawyer.

Law school was a four-year blur of stress and anxiety. I was often dizzy for months at a time. We had additional children. Abigail underwent additional brain surgeries. I shuttled from the children's hospital to school to a job I held doing work for oil companies. I also began publishing on conservative and traditional Catholic weblogs, although I knew that it would end any hopes I had of an academic career, even teaching at community colleges as I had done in the past. Unlike Michael, I knew well enough that as a conservative an academic career would have been difficult at best. Writing for publication or speaking my mind would make it completely impossible.

The main thing I learned from my four years of law school, my postgraduate year working at a law firm, and spending so much time with doctors, was that law school and medical school are glorified trade schools; as we will acknowledge in this book, these tradesmen are some of the only folks who actually need their degrees. But such tradesmen, given the grave responsibilities they execute, desperately need (though they might not know it) a real education that they lack: grounding in the teachings of Aristotle and Saint Thomas Aquinas.

Accordingly, after a year in the law, I returned to teaching at the Catholic high school in California where I'd taught prior to our move to Rome; I wanted to give students a grounding in great Catholic ideas and thinkers that they would not otherwise get (and that no one, including myself, had been getting in the 1970s, 1980s, 1990s, or 2000s). Situated in a politically conservative enclave, I had once been popular there, and the school was pleased to give me my teaching job back—especially now that I had attained two additional graduate degrees that they could use to boast about their faculty. Shortly thereafter, the school made me the theology department chairman, and simultaneously my public profile grew as I wrote my first few books and became a popular Catholic commentator.

During the 2020 summer of Black Lives Matter riots, the high school's woke leftist alumni—most of whom I had never taught—circulated a petition to get me fired for speaking out publicly against the domestic terrorism taking over American cities. They succeeded in their efforts, and I realized that a right winger could not even teach at a Catholic school in a conservative part of California. By the way, that incident became something of a cause célèbre because of its implications for free speech and because of the drama of its occurring when my daughter had recently undergone her most extensive brain surgery to date. It ended with a move to Mississippi from my home state and setting myself up as an independent author, lecturer, and commentator—and meeting Michael Robillard.

Here's the point: through the providence of God, Michael and I narrowly managed to escape all the many pitfalls that typically surround college students, especially ones who remain in the academy for multiple graduate degrees. We've told you so much about ourselves in order to impart this much: our college experiences were in many ways utterly atypical. But we also saw what *was typical* as we progressed through our university careers, and we recognized that the vast majority of people would be better off *never* going to college. We also learned how we could uniquely reach and teach graduating high-school seniors—via books, podcasts, and even extracurricular Zoom classes—all the worthy things that most colleges refuse to teach.

The bottom line is that college isn't necessary for you to thrive.

In fact, for most people, it is an expensive way to buy debt, smug ignorance, and unhappiness.

So, let the revolution—for truth, beauty, and intellectual freedom—begin. Don't go to college. If you're in college, drop out, get a job, get married, and educate yourself with thematic content on par with the notes of this book. If you *must* go to college—and we recognize that a minority of people must in order to become doctors or lawyers or engineers—then we have some advice for you too on how to lead the revolution from inside the beast and make the most of your time.

CHAPTER TWO

Wokeism 101

"Too much of what is called 'education' is little more than an expensive isolation from reality."

—Thomas Sowell

We could lead with the economic argument against college, but we'll save that for the next chapter. Because, arguably, it would be worth going into debt if you were receiving something truly valuable in return. But in most cases you won't be—and the reason for this is that almost every college or university has been taken over by professors and an administration whose primary goal is to indoctrinate you into a hyper-potent new strain of Marxism. This is the reason why we need a counterrevolution in higher education.

Indeed, examples of growing campus intolerance, extremism, and insanity are now legion. You've probably read or at least heard about some of the major ones. You likely, however, have not heard of the more bizarre or fringe instances, many of which have occurred just within the last five years alone, nor have you heard of the central theory animating all of this madness. For that you must understand the fundamental ideology that has utterly absorbed present-day higher education. It is the explanation for all of the insanity. It is called *intersectionality.* If you go to college, you will be immersed in it—and no one in their right mind should want to be.

What the Heck Is Intersectionality?

Intersectionality, first coined by feminist-Marxist Kimberlé Crenshaw in 1989, is a theory that conceives certain persons and groups as being discriminated against, oppressed, or unjustly marginalized along an intersecting and overlapping set of axes, features, and criteria. What intersectionality really does is take age-old human vices—like self-pity, envy, and power-hunger—and weaponize them in the language of grievance and victimhood that is so seductive to Marxists and the enduring Marxist subculture.

If this were a game—and in some ways it is—the goal would be to accumulate the most "minority" status grievance points. For example, a black woman who is disabled might be marginalized *in part* because of her race, *in part* because she is female, and *in part* because of her disability, and the *aggregation* of these features means she has been marginalized and deserves redress, *even if there is no explicit law or social rule discriminating against her.* To become "woke" under this logic is to become consciously aware of how we—as individuals, groups, or institutions—contribute to and unjustly benefit from these alleged invisible systems of intersectional oppression. Proponents of intersectionality argue that oppressed persons are thereby entitled to certain public goods or positions of power and that non-oppressed persons and groups (heterosexual, white male Christians most of all) have a corresponding positive duty to accommodate them.

The tacit assumption is that disparities in institutional power and privilege are inherently unearned and inherently unfair and that any disparity in power or privilege is the result of some form of past or present injustice that we are duty bound to undo through gradual institutional reform or by swift revolutionary action. What the woke call "equity" (equality of outcome, not opportunity) is a moral requirement; and a speaker's "lived experience" and overall standing in the intersectional hierarchy take precedence over all else. Any other morally relevant features like nature, capability, merit, virtue, dignity, well-being, fairness, liberty, autonomy, duty, decency, validity, or truth—all things that a true university would teach and value—are disregarded.

As a moral system, intersectionality is ridiculous and perverse. But that has not stopped it from becoming completely dominant in our universities and other institutions. In practice, by demonizing the most successful and productive groups and attacking America's (and the West's) foundations, traditions, and heritage, intersectionality is simply a kind of malignant parasitism. In the short term, those who wield intersectionality profit from it. In the long term, intersectionality must destroy the successful civilization on which it feeds.

The Big Four Intersectionalities on Campus

Colleges and universities have their own shibboleths that have rapidly filtered down to the general culture, to include words and phrases like *diversity, equity, and inclusion*; *problematic language*; *unconscious racial bias*; *patriarchy*; *checking one's privilege*; *anti-racism*; *anti-whiteness* (a "good" thing by the way); *toxic masculinity*; *safe spaces*; *trigger-warnings*; *white fragility*; *microaggressions*; *bigotry*; *and phobias*, along with ritualistic apologies for college campuses *being on stolen land* and the now ubiquitous presence of the rainbow-LGBTQ+ and Black Lives Matter flags. These are all surface expressions of intersectionality's all-consuming ideological hegemony. Most often on campus it can be grouped under four headings: "Anti-Colonialism," Critical Race Theory (CRT), Feminism, and LGBTQ+.

Anti-Colonialism

"Anti-colonialism" is a doctrine that argues that because of the transatlantic slave trade (generally upheld as the worst crime in human history and requiring infinite redress), the conquest of Native American tribes, and European imperialism, present-day descendants of Europeans are morally obligated to make reparations for presumed past injustices. In Britain and America, this has become the excuse for the iconoclastic frenzy of statue toppling and building renaming to remove any honor given to anyone who was in any way connected to territorial conquest or the slave trade or who is imputed with ever uttering anything even vaguely associable with "white racism." By the way, the latter constitutes a category so obscenely expansive that it includes everyone from Christopher Columbus and Thomas Jefferson to Robert E. Lee, Mark Twain, Cecil Rhodes, Paula Deen, and Morgan Wallen. Similarly, on American, Canadian, Australian, and New Zealand campuses it is now commonplace for administrators to acknowledge that their campuses are built on so-called "stolen land." It is routine for university literature, history, and social-science programs to "de-colonize the curriculum" by throwing out or deemphasizing much of what a truly educated person should know solely because it is "European," or was written by a white man, or highlights European accomplishments that might date anywhere from ancient Greece through the Roman Empire to British colonialism and subsequent American history. And, of course, students and graduates who can claim African or "indigenous" ancestry are often rewarded with special rules, sinecures, and privileges on account of their "minority" status.

Interestingly, in higher education in the United States, Asians are sometimes discriminated *against* by the woke regime because they are too successful vis à vis other "intersectional" groups. In fact, the academic success of Asian students, as with Jewish students before them (in 1922, 21 percent of Harvard's freshmen were Jewish[1]), is something of an embarrassment to the woke, intersectional, academic authorities. It implies that the "dominant white culture" isn't so prejudiced against minorities, after all. It's actually the liberal college administrators who discriminate against academically *successful* minorities. As Kenny Xu reports in his article "Harvard's Diversity Disgrace" in the *Spectator World*:

> According to 90,000 pages of Harvard admissions data, an Asian-American student must score 450 points higher on the SAT to have the same chance of admission as a black student with the same qualifications.... Without discrimination, Asian Americans would make up 43 percent of the Harvard student body [rather than 15 to 20 percent], according to Harvard's own Office of Institutional Research.[2]

Beyond this, a disproportionate number of Harvard's admitted black students come from wealthy households—71 percent of black admissions are "upper middle class or higher."[3] By contrast, "many Asian-American applicants are from first- or second-generation immigrant families."[4]

Critical Race Theory (CRT)

Critical race theory closely overlaps with "anti-colonialism." First developed in the 1970s as an offshoot of critical legal theory, CRT at its heart is pretty much the complete antithesis of Martin Luther King Jr.'s professed dream of a race-blind society. Under CRT, racial identity takes priority over all else.

As CRT theorist Kimberlé Crenshaw puts it, CRT is more of a verb than a noun. She writes: "It is a way of seeing, attending to, accounting for, tracing and analyzing the ways that race is produced, the ways that racial inequality is facilitated, and the ways that our history has created these inequalities that now can be almost effortlessly reproduced unless we attend to the existence of these inequalities."[5]

In a similar vein, CRT proponent Mari Matsuda says: "For me critical race theory is a method that takes the lived experience of racism seriously, using history and social reality to explain how racism operates in American law and culture, toward the end of eliminating the harmful effects of racism and bringing about a just and healthy world for all."[6]

CRT leapt into the limelight with the *New York Times*–sponsored 1619 Project, which put slavery at the center of American history. (One critical response to the 1619 Project was the 1776 Report of the President's Advisory 1776 Commission in January 2021.[7]) CRT appeared in newspapers and news shows across the country with the meteoric rise of the radical Marxist group, Black Lives Matter. CRT is becoming institutionalized in mandatory training in "diversity, equity, and inclusion," "anti-racism," and "anti-whiteness" in a growing number of universities, colleges, and corporate settings. And it has been popularized in books like Robin DiAngelo's *White Fragility* and Ibram X. Kendi's *How to Be an Antiracist*.[8] To quote Kendi:

> The opposite of racist isn't "not racist." It is "antiracist." What's the difference? One endorses either the idea of a racial hierarchy as a racist, or racial equality as an antiracist. One either believes problems are rooted in groups of people, as a racist, or locates the roots of problems in power and policies, as an antiracist. One either allows racial inequities to persevere, as a racist, or confronts racial

inequities, as an antiracist. There is no in-between safe space of "not racist."[9]

To put that into plain language, CRT treats the idea of a color-blind society with contempt. Boiled down, CRT is committed to three core tenets: that one is defined by one's racial group identity; that because of "systemic" and "institutional" racism, whites have a kind of secular original sin for which they must be ongoingly punished and discriminated against; and that government and other institutions are morally obligated to make reparations for and undo racial oppression—and racial oppression exists in practically everything (including, as we'll see later, mathematics). Martin Luther King Jr. couched his civil-rights crusade in the language of Christianity and the ideals of the American founding. CRT, by contrast, is motivated by desires for vengeance and profit and animated by hate and anti-white racial discrimination.

Feminism

Feminism is the oldest branch of intersectionality. Its adherents often refer to four separate "waves" of feminism, dating back to the eighteenth century. Even if feminism is "the rolling revolution," as scholar Scott Yennor calls it,[10] both the goals and the results of feminism over the centuries prove to be pretty clear and consistent (and have been gaining momentum): destroying the nuclear family, decreasing the rate of marriage and increasing beyond the limits of fertility the average age of wedlock, and vituperating Western birth rates—all things, incidentally, that correlate with loneliness, depression, and unhappiness. The radicalism of feminism, its deleterious effects, and its subtle conceptual links to the current "gender" insanity are often widely underestimated. Still, feminism has VIP status at college and ubiquitously enjoys its own "women's studies" department at almost every campus in the land. The tensions, however, between a fundamentally anti-Christian ideology based on the alleged historical oppression of women by men and the new "transgender" movement, which argues that male and female constitute nothing more than social constructs that can be chosen at will, are problematic to say the least. And when even wildly popular liberal-feminist authors like J. K. Rowling are criticized, denounced, and blacklisted for denying that men can be women, it would seem that the future doesn't look good on campus for so-called TERFs (trans-exclusionary-radical-feminists). Nonetheless, feminism has proven to be the oldest and sturdiest intersectional sin against those of good will, and one shouldn't expect it to go anywhere anytime soon.

LGBTQ+

The newest and most radical expression of intersectionality comes from the now well-known Lesbian, Gay, Bisexual, Transgender, and Queer "community," with the plus sign at the end representing a never-ending revolution of weaponized, gender-dysphoric "identities."

You might have heard of them.

With nearly every major media, academic, governmental, corporate, military, and religious institution now vocally and enthusiastically on their side, and with *three* whole calendar months (and counting) officially dedicated to their cause,[11] these scrappy underdog freedom fighters somehow continue to keep bucking the establishment and "speaking truth to power" against nearly impossible odds. How do they do it? All joking aside, what was pitched to the American public as a set of claims designed to protect homosexuals from being harmed, killed, or persecuted in some kind of Matthew Shepard–type event (which turned out to be fabricated anyhow)[12] has been unmasked as a movement of aggressively advancing sexual perversion such as the world has never known, fast approaching the unmitigated normalization of pederasty, bestiality, and necrophilia. The LGBTQ+ mafia now exercises near total hegemonic domination over every single major institution within the Western world, to include increasingly monopolistic control over our language—and therefore to what our society asserts as truth itself. They also are apparently recruiting vast numbers of young people into their ranks, with the percentage of the American population claiming to be LGBTQ+ more than doubling since 2012, driven in large part by a shocking near–16 percent of Generation Z (born between 1997 and 2012) claiming to be LGBTQ+ (compared to 3.5 percent of the general population in 2012).[13] Indeed, "the subversive homosexual agenda" constituting a grooming-recruitment program that grandpa and all those "Christian right-wing extremists" used to rant about turned out to be real. But even the late Phyllis Schlafly and the late Jerry Falwell would likely be surprised at the sheer speed, magnitude, and scope with which this radical movement has swept over America's institutions.

Even today, few understand how revolutionary the homosexual agenda has been, molesting our sense of biology, nature, procreation, freedom, the family, reason, natural law, morality, tolerance, and truth. One of the few is Marek Jędraszewski, the Catholic Archbishop of Kraków. In a 2019 speech marking the seventy-fifth anniversary of the Warsaw Uprising against the National Socialists, he noted that while the Poles had freed themselves from Nazi tyranny and then from Communist tyranny, a new tyranny had presented itself. "A red plague is not gripping our land anymore, which does not mean that there is not a new one that wants to control our souls, hearts, and minds.... Not Marxist, Bolshevik, but born of the same spirit, neo-Marxist.... Not red, but rainbow." The Poles, he said, had fought to defend their faith and the sanctity of their families from atheistic communism. Now they had to defend them from an ideology with absolutist demands that denied basic truths about human beings, human dignity, and the integrity of male and female.[14] Or, as Professor Carl Trueman of Grove City College puts it,

> There is a clear push to grant LGBTQ+ ideology a favored legal and cultural status that enforces it without compromise. It also labels any and all dissent as morally evil. You don't have to be an Old Testament prophet to see where this is all heading, or at least where those in power hope it is heading.... to the comprehensive destabilizing of society.... The family must be dismantled; biology must fall to gender ideology; dissenters must be discredited and vilified.[15]

The lightning-fast emergence of the LGBTQ+ movement is, in fact, a perfect example of how one thing leads to another without most people even recognizing what happened. The sexual revolution of the 1960s led to four decades of aggressively destigmatizing sexual perversity of every stripe. The unadorned homosexual agenda first appeared in American culture in the early to mid-2000's (circa 2005), culminating with the successful passage of the California ballot proposition, "Prop 8," banning same-sex marriage but being overturned in court. That led to the legalization of same-sex marriage in 2015 and the near-instant explosion of "transgenderism"—something that almost every American had previously never even heard about, or cared about. Consider such moral incrementalism in view of this frightening logarithmic curve: feminism—the view that male and female are functionally fungible within the family—required from 1848 until the 1950's to gain popular American acceptance, roughly one hundred years (ten squared); homosexualism—the view that male and female are sexually fungible in the bedroom—required from around 2005 until 2015 to gain popular acceptance, roughly ten years (that is, ten to the first power); transsexualism—the view that if, in the context of the family or the bedroom, men can *act like* women and vice versa, they can actually *be* women—took a mere one year (ten to the zeroth power) to percolate in the American culture before being rolled out prefabricated and readily applied to everything. Sometime between 2013 and 2015, we all heard about the gender dysphoria of Bruce Jenner, and then the rest was history. In fact, the "trans" movement has now taken center stage and deserves a subhead of its own.

"Trans" Rights

Ironically—since they may soon be enemies, if they aren't already—it was feminism that birthed the trans movement. It arose out of the sex/gender distinction of Simone de Beauvoir's *Second Sex* in 1949 and later from Judith Butler's expanded musings on "gender" in her work *Gender Trouble* in the 1990s. Since then, the ideology of "gender" and hence, "transgender," has spread with unprecedented speed (especially considering its radicalism) throughout both academia and the world at large.

The *Stanford Encyclopedia for Philosophy* entry on "Feminist Perspectives on Sex and Gender," for instance, captures the conceptual distinction between "sex" and "gender" as follows:

> Many feminists...have endorsed the sex/gender distinction. Provisionally: "sex" denotes human females and males depending on *biological* features (chromosomes, sex organs, hormones and other physical features); "gender" denotes women and men depending on *social* factors (social role, position, behaviour or identity). The main feminist

motivation for making this distinction was to counter biological determinism or the view that biology is destiny.[16]

Judith Butler, in *Gender Trouble*, echoes this distinction writing
that "Gender is not to culture as sex is to nature; gender is also the
discursive/cultural means by which 'sexed nature' or 'a natural sex'
is produced and established as 'prediscursive,' prior to culture, a politically neutral surface on which culture acts."[17]

And lastly, the World Health Organization rearticulates this
conceptual distinction between "sex" and "gender" while making the
further distinction between "gender" and "gender identity," stating
the following:

> Gender refers to the characteristics of women, men, girls
> and boys that are socially constructed. This includes
> norms, behaviours and roles associated with being a
> woman, man, girl or boy, as well as relationships with each
> other. As a social construct, gender varies from society to
> society and can change over time.... Gender interacts with
> but is different from sex, which refers to the different bio-
> logical and physiological characteristics of females, males
> and intersex persons, such as chromosomes, hormones and
> reproductive organs. Gender and sex are related to but dif-
> ferent from gender identity. Gender identity refers to a
> person's deeply felt, internal and individual experience of
> gender, which may or may not correspond to the person's
> physiology or designated sex at birth.[18]

As you can tell by trying to read that passage, until recently the
idea of a sex/gender distinction was largely relegated to feminist academic departments and the institutions over which they had influence.

But again, the bad ideas that get started and supported on universities don't stay there, beginning insidiously with language, where feminists were successful in pushing out the word "sex" for "gender" in many people's speech and on official forms. Few understood what that meant or where they were heading. Now, of course, the activists are going even further with the distinction between "sex" and "gender" by claiming that "transgender women *are* women" and that those who don't acknowledge this blatant falsehood—just as those who refused to acknowledge make-believe pronouns before—should be punished. To "misgender" someone, to not use one's "preferred pronouns," to not honor a person's subjectively determined (and changeable) gender identity, constitutes not just grave disrespect, in the transgenderist view, but "violence."[19]

Truth is a casualty of all this. In her article "In Defense of Transracialism," philosopher Rebecca Tuvel notes: "Generally, we treat people wrongly when we block them from assuming the personal identity they wish to assume."[20] In other words, we're supposed to deny reality and affirm someone's desire to live in a fantasy world. Furthermore, as transgenderist philosophers Daniel Wodak and Robin Dembroff argue in their article "He/She/They/Ze":

> We have a negative duty not to use binary gender-specific pronouns (*he* or *she*) to refer to genderqueer individuals. We defend this with an argument by analogy. It was gravely wrong for Mark Latham to refer to Catherine McGregor, a transgender woman, using the pronoun *he*; we argue that such cases of misgendering are morally analogous to referring to Angel Haze, who identifies as genderqueer, as *he* or *she*. The second is a radical claim: we have a negative duty not to use any gender-specific pronouns to refer to anyone, regardless of their gender identity.[21]

Yeah, we don't understand any of this nonsense either. But remember, *it's all a psy-op*, one you will be subjected to *especially closely* if you go to college, one that is intended to make you affirm flat—not to mention bizarre—untruths, deny reality and, by the way, renounce any Christian or conservative beliefs you might have.

+ *Rights*

In the transgenderist view, the "T" in LGBT is already an *infinite* claim, but just to make sure that we all understand this, the generally approved acronym has become LGBTQ+ for good measure. Even so, it is not unusual, especially in university settings, to see at least a half dozen more letters thrown into the identitarian "alphabet soup" of gender dysphoria. For instance, there is LGBTQQIAAP+ (which tacks on "queer," "questioning," "intersex," "asexual," "agender," and "poly"). Mind you, these are all ostensibly *equally* competing rights claims as well. What's more, by these folks' own account, there is no logical reason whatsoever to stop there.

The "+" sign is a conceptual placeholder for literally any and all future "marginalized" groups imaginable, no matter how niche, bizarre, vicious, contradictory, illogical, incoherent, or detrimental to individuals and civilization as a whole. Indeed, the weirder and more niche, and therefore the more marginalized, *the better*. There is even now emerging advocacy for pedophiles, rebranded as MAPs ("minor attracted persons"). Just slap the word "rights" onto the end of it, and they're off to the races. The progression of these supposed "rights" claims is predictable, a one-way ratchet effect: from social de-stigmatization to greater and greater social normalization, to mandatory social celebration, to legal normalization, to social and then legal persecution of opponents.

The "+" sign in "LGBTQ+" functions in essence as a kind of metaphysical aperture torn and left wide open in the fabric of the social universe; and this aperature now serves (and will continue to serve, if not plugged very soon) as a never-ending font of ever-expanding emergent-victim groups, perpetually replenishing the ranks of the professionally offended and giving ever wider latitude to social, cultural, and legal insanity.

The Wrong Side of History

To raise any objections to any of this in an academic setting is difficult at best, because the academy takes it as a truism that what is new is always better than what is old, that "equity" for every "marginalized" group is a moral imperative, and that history is marching inevitably in a progressive, leftist direction of ever-greater egalitarianism. The academy generally labels those who oppose such leftism as on "the wrong side of history" and guilty of ignorance and bigotry. Really, it is a tactic to shut off debate. As Noam Chomsky once wrote:

> The smart way to keep people passive and obedient is to strictly limit the spectrum of acceptable opinion, but allow very lively debate within that spectrum—even encourage the more critical and dissident views. That gives people the sense that there's free thinking going on, while all the time the presuppositions of the system are being reinforced by the limits put on the range of the debate.[22]

He meant that as criticism of American society, but it's really a peek at the playbook of academia. All the various progressive initiatives, speech codes, and intersectional analyses that preponderate in academia prove to be, in essence, a means to limit debate within a leftist framework. To be blunt, it is communism by another name—updated so that its Marxist focus on socialism and class is expanded to race, feminism, "gender," and other leftist enthusiasms—and "liberals" are unwilling to stop it, in part because these neo-Marxists adopt (and pervert) "liberal" language. Indeed, as American Communist activist Alexander Trachtenberg noted at the National Convention for Communist Parties in 1944:

> When we get ready to take the United States, we will not take it under the label of Communism, we will not take it under the label of Socialism. These labels are unpleasant to the American people.... We will take the United States under labels we have made very lovable! We will take it under "Liberalism," under "Progressivism," under "Democracy" but take it we will![23]

Nowhere have these infiltrators triumphed more than in our colleges and universities, which have become neo-Marxist indoctrination centers advancing the very same agenda and using the very same linguistic tricks as Trachtenberg suggested. Critical race theory is taught in mandatory programs at more than 230 colleges and universities throughout the United States,[24] and its influence covers the gamut, including hiring criteria.[25]

Movements to "decolonize" the curriculum are sweeping over an alarming number of elite colleges and universities. In June 2021, Princeton University eliminated its Greek and Latin requirements for *classics* majors in the name of combating "systemic racism." In fall 2020, at Brown University, the student group "Decolonization at Brown" (DAB) lobbied to remove the statues of Roman emperors Marcus Aurelius and Caesar Augustus from campus; DAB argued that the statues were harmful to students because "they celebrate the ongoing occupation of Native land by the United States and replace Native histories with monuments to white, Western civilization."

"In a close vote, Brown's student government rejected DAB's plea to remove the statues," but the university said it still intended to relocate them (showing that even when *someone* stands up to the radicals, college administrations often won't). According to the National Association of Scholars, as of 2010, "only 32 percent of America's 50 most elite schools offered courses on Western civilization, and none of the colleges and universities required them."[26]

In the 2022 article "How Our Universities Became Sheep Factories," Cambridge professor of philosophy Arif Ahmed chronicles a very similar "woke" takeover of his own university and of British higher education in general. He notes, "The very purpose of a university is being redefined. You might think [universities] exist to conduct teaching and research. That would be naïve. Most universities now routinely call themselves *anti-racist institutions*, where this means: actively campaigning for a political end."[27]

American colleges and universities have had a strong left-wing bias for decades. But there is growing evidence that an extreme leftward lurch is being navigated in academia. A 2006 survey conducted by psychologist Jonathan Haidt and sociologist Solon Simmons found that only 14 percent of professors self-identified as "conservative."[28] A 2020 National Association of Scholars (NAS) report on leading institutions of higher education found that the Democrat-to-Republican ratio among professors is 9:1 and increases to 11:1 for young professors. For female professors the ratio is 16:1. And within the humanities and social sciences, the ratios are a staggering 42.2:1 in anthropology, 27:1 in sociology, and 26.8:1 in English. Perhaps even more telling, the same NAS report noted a staggering *95:1 ratio* between liberal and conservative professors when it came to donorship towards political parties.[29] Not only do liberals and leftists dominate higher education, they are also far more activist when it comes to politics.

This spills over into what many conservative professors would regard as extreme hostility to their opinions—if they chose to express them. In a 2016 survey titled, *Passing on the Right: Conservative Professors in the Progressive University*, Jon Shields and Joshua Dunn interviewed 153 self-described "conservative" professors and found that one-third admitted to attempting to hide or deny their political views because of an inhospitable work environment.[30] Maybe that's why it seems to be easier to find conservative academics at think tanks rather than at universities.

If professors feel this pressure to conform and hide their views—and if they are abandoning academia for think tanks, which, anecdotally, seems to be the case—how abandoned must conservative students feel? And ask yourself, why should you—or your parents—pay to be forced to endure such indoctrination? The fact is, you shouldn't. If you think going to college will sharpen your intellect and make you a critical thinker, you're going to the wrong place. Our universities insist on and reward neo-Marxist conformity. You think you're going to be reading Great Books? Think again. They're getting purged from the curriculum as racist and colonialist. You can get a classics degree from an Ivy League university without knowing Greek or Latin. You can get an English degree without reading Shakespeare. And if by some good fortune you are assigned, say, a classic novel, odds are you'll be asked to apply a feminist-Marxist–anti-colonialist theory to it in order to "deconstruct" it. When it comes to economics, don't be surprised if the failure of socialism in practice hasn't dented its appeal to your left-wing professors. Even in the sciences, as we'll see, the neo-Marxists are beginning to exert their hegemony in ways that have a very bad historical track record.

Leftist intellectuals see you as a captive audience. They don't understand that there's more to life than school—and more to life than writing Ph.D. dissertations about how many men can birth babies on the head of a pin. Leftist intellectuals can embrace crazy ideas because they meet no real-world test. As Thomas Sowell rightly notes, intellectuals are "people whose end products are ideas.... If [an engineer] builds a building that collapses, it doesn't matter how brilliant his idea was, he's ruined. Conversely, if an intellectual who is brilliant has an idea for rearranging society, and that ends in disaster, he pays no price at all."[31]

What does this mean for you, as you contemplate going to college? It means you can count on spending four to six years of your life stuffing your head full of garbage and propaganda, taught to you by people who know surprisingly little, who hate everything you believe, and whose hefty salaries you'll be paying while they work to undermine your formerly Christian society with their subversive ideas. Or you can get on with your life. You can go on to trade school, apprentice yourself to a craftsman, become an entrepreneur, or commit yourself to any of a hundred other things such as working as an actor, a delivery driver, a florist, a personal trainer, a salesman, a chef, or a real estate agent. You might even see the world as a merchant seaman. As one friend of ours told us:

> I did *not* go to college after high school. This was a radical and shocking decision for my family, as well as for my high school teachers. I was smart enough and a good student. But I hated high school. With the exception of one rigorous and intellectually tough English teacher, high school seemed like such a waste of time, a great distraction from real life. From books I devoured on my own time, I was on fire for adventure and the desire to go to sea, and to see the world. I saved all my money from working as a busboy and laborer in a boat yard so that when I graduated, I bought a one-way ticket to the U.S. Virgin Islands.... While I did not see it

this way at the time, what I had in fact done was throw myself into a maritime apprenticeship program, where I literally learned the ropes of seamanship with a variety of captains who had a profound effect on my life. Before I was twenty years old, I had survived a hurricane while living afloat, lost everything I owned in a boat fire in Martinique, done my first trans-Atlantic passage, and actually gotten paid to see some incredible places. And all those days at sea would count as legally documentable sea time for when I would eventually get my 100-ton master's license years later.... The best decision of my life (besides marrying my wife) was *not* going to college when I was a lad on fire. Getting a useful trade has been a deep and very real blessing.... The credential I am most proud of and grateful for is my captain's license, and I have that because I ran away to sea when I was young.

Science-fiction writer Robert Heinlein once wrote that "A human being should be able to change a diaper, plan an invasion, butcher a hog, conn a ship, design a building, write a sonnet, balance accounts, build a wall, set a bone, comfort the dying, take orders, give orders, cooperate, act alone, solve equations, analyze a new problem, pitch manure, program a computer, cook a tasty meal, fight efficiently, die gallantly."[32] You likely won't learn many of those things in college. Instead, when not being lectured on gender and racism, you'll be encouraged to choose a major and then attend graduate school, honing yourself in some academic specialization. But, as Heinlein concludes, "Specialization is for insects."[33] A much better way to go is to teach yourself—and teaching yourself, becoming an autodidact, has never been easier, with the world's library available to you at the punch of a button and free online courses offered at schools like

Hillsdale College,[34] and inexpensive courses on technical subjects at places like Coursera.[35] Other liberal arts options include the Ignatius-Angelicum Great Books Program that operates in conjunction with Holy Apostles College and advertises itself as "the cure for the college debt crisis"[36] and Catholic Distance University.[37] You'll find more reading recommendations throughout this book. If you can read, you can teach yourself. So do it.

There's much more to life than school. And college is *anything but* a life requirement. As we'll show in the next chapter, for most students college is not just morally and intellectually degrading, it's a bad investment. In fact, it's not an investment at all—it's merely a way of enriching the Marxist revolutionaries who hate your faith, your family, and your flag.

CHAPTER THREE

The Cost of College:
Why College Is Bad for Your Wallet

"Growing up, I was told, since I was a child, that your destiny is to go to college.
That is what is going to lift our family up and out."

—Alexandria Ocasio-Cortez

According to a January 2022 "Average Cost of College & Tuition" report from Education Data Initiative,

- The average annual cost for a student attending a four-year college is $35,331 (including books, supplies, and living expenses)
- The average annual cost for a student attending an in-state four-year public university is $25,487
- The average annual cost for a community college is $7,460 total or $1,865 per semester
- Over the last twenty years, average college costs have more than doubled
- Average Cost of Law School is $205,744
- Average Cost of Medical School is $218,792
- Average Cost of a Doctorate degree is $114,300
- Average Cost of a Master's degree is $66,340
- Average Cost of College Textbooks is $1,240[1]

But the most important number is this: "Considering student loan interest and loss of income [from what one could have earned from working full-time], the ultimate cost of a bachelor's degree can exceed $400,000."[2]

Who, in their right minds, thinks a bachelor's degree is worth $400,000?

Even if the education you received was of premium quality, that's an insane number. But more likely the college education you'll receive will be an even worse waste of your time and money than that number suggests. As Mike Rowe—entrepreneur and host of the television show *Dirty Jobs*—has noted: "The cost of college has grown faster than the cost of energy and the cost of real estate, the cost of healthcare. All of it. Somehow we got it into our heads that it's priceless."[3] Guess what? It's not. Or as the joke goes, "Thank you student loans for helping me get through college. I don't think I can ever repay you." Or, as Alexandria Ocasio-Cortez recently proclaimed:

> This is ridiculous. I am 32 years old. I'm a first-generation college graduate on my mom's side, and growing up I was told, since I was a child: "Your destiny is to go to college. That's what's gonna lift our family up and out. That is our future. That's what we are here to accomplish." Seventeen years old when college recruiters started coming to my high school saying, "this is worth it." And we still do that today, because it's teenagers signing up for what is often hundreds of thousands of dollars of debt, and we just do that. And our government allows that.
>
> We give seventeen-year-olds the ability to sign on and sign up for a hundred thousand dollars' worth of debt, and we think that is responsible policy. I'm thirty-two years old now. I have over seventeen thousand dollars in student loan

debt, and I didn't go to graduate school because I knew that getting another degree would drown me in debt that I would never be able to surpass. This is unacceptable. Not only that: 65 percent of all jobs in this country require an education beyond high school. First generation college students are two times as likely to report being behind on student loan payments. And 63 percent of borrowers who made payments with Naviance during the COVID forbearance still owe more now than they originally borrowed. There are hundreds of thousands of people in this country who owe more on their student loans now than they did when they first took them out. We as a country are profiting off of insurmountable and crushing educational debt and it is wrong. It is absolutely wrong.[4]

The student-loan problem is not a left-right issue. The Left might have wrong answers on how to deal with it. Their answer is debt "forgiveness" and "free" college for everyone, which, if it means anything, means sticking taxpayers with an unbelievably exorbitant bill of more than $2 trillion. Those are taxpayers who are already getting fleeced to subsidize state colleges and universities to indoctrinate the next generation with the notion that men can have babies.

But at least those on the Left don't deny that an aggregate national student-loan debt of $1,930,446,972,357 (as of February 15, 2022) is a problem—a problem that is, by the way, accruing interest at approximately $3,000 per second.[5] According to financial expert Dave Ramsey, in 2019 American families borrowed more than $106 billion for college. After twelve years, the average collegiate borrower has only paid off about a third of his student loan. The average borrower pays off his student loan in around 30 years.[6] In other words, taking out a student loan for college is the rough equivalent of taking out a loan for a house. In fact, the median price of a house in 2021 was $374,900—$50,000 more than the year before,[7] yet still $25,000 *less* than the estimated ultimate cost of a bachelor's degree.

In contrast to the Left's irresponsible call for writing off student loans, Madison Cawthorn, a young Republican congressman from North Carolina, has a more responsible take:

> I am proudly a college dropout. If you are not becoming an engineer or a doctor or a lawyer, I highly encourage you to drop out. It's a scam.... Instead of taking out that $100,000...student loan as an eighteen-year-old, which is worthless as an eighteen-year-old, why doesn't the government allow us to be able to take out a $10,000 business loan at eighteen to be able to go and create an economy and create work and create all these great things.[8]

There is certainly much more ingenuity and good created by young entrepreneurs providing services and jobs than there is in any number of indebted grievance-studies majors sitting in dorms eating Cheetos and worrying about getting fat-shamed. There is a ton more value in the work done by plumbers, bricklayers, electricians, and roofers than there is by graduates with senior theses on gender roles. Instead of wasting four to six years in college, those construction and housing workers were likely trained on the job, earning money rather than acquiring debt while providing a valuable service. Skilled workers in the private sector are the truly productive people in our society. They're the ones who support everything else, including America's financially rapacious colleges and universities that should be defunded now. With a trade, and without college debt, you can get on with your life. Young, skilled workers can be truly free, financially and intellectually, in a way that indebted and indoctrinated former college students aren't.

Follow the Money

As one wit told us, "The only people who give out $100,000 loans to 18-year-olds are loan sharks—and student loan companies." Unlike business loans, private student loans can't be discharged through bankruptcy. For most young people, starting out in their careers, student loans are a millstone around their necks. Student loan companies make outrageous profits from these millstones, and so do college and university administrators. The average college president is paid $309,889 a year,[9] with some making well over $2,000,000.[10] In higher education the rich get richer, as universities make a point of hiring "celebrity" professors or lecturers when they can. Democrat senator Elizabeth Warren of Massachusetts, for instance, was paid $429,981 to be a guest lecturer at Harvard in 2010 and 2011 (ostensibly to lecture about economic inequality).[11] In 2017 the University of Pennsylvania hired then former vice president Joe Biden as its "Benjamin Franklin Presidential Practice Professor." He was paid $776,527 and never had to teach a single course. At the time, "the average annual salary for everyday full professors at Penn—excluding high-earners like doctors who don't usually teach—was $214,000."[12] When "everyday full professors" are making more than $200,000, you know there's a lot of money sloshing around. How many people do you know earning more than $200,000; and how many of them work leisurely academic schedules?

Public universities are notorious not just for indebting their students and draining money from students' parents, but for splashing taxpayer dollars on boondoggle academic conferences, which allow feminist literature professors to travel the country talking about the hidden themes of patriarchy and racism and heteronormativism in *Moby Dick*. For some academics, sometimes even those boondoggles are not enough. One California State University San Marcos dean came under investigation after whistleblowers found that the university had spent $82,000 on his lavish, luxury-end international travel.[13] Moreover, an April 2017 state audit of the University of California system "revealed that the Office of the President had 'amassed substantial reserve funds, used misleading budgeting practices, provided its employees with generous salaries and atypical benefits, and failed to satisfactorily justify its spending on systemwide initiatives.'" Additionally, "between fiscal years 2012–13 and 2015–16, the Office of the President's administrative spending increased by 28%, or $80 million. And 10 executives in the office whose salaries were analyzed by the audit made a total of $3.7 million in FY2014—$700,000 more than the combined salaries of their highest-paid state employee counterparts."[14]

They thought they could get away with it, because, you know, it's all about education—a sacred cow, if ever there was one.

In the last twenty-five years, according to a 2014 HuffPost article, "the number of non-academic administrative and professional employees at U.S. colleges and universities has more than doubled...vastly outpacing the growth in the number of students or faculty, according to an analysis of federal figures."[15] In 2022, the *San Jose Mercury News* reported that Mills College in northern California spent more on campus administration than on instruction.[16] Of course, the ideology of intersectionality helps drive administrative spending upward because it requires the hiring of ever more diversity, equity, and inclusion commissars. Ohio State, for example, has what one observer called "a small army of 132 'diversicrats.'" Their "total estimated payroll cost" is $13.4 million, including $289,600 going to an "Associate Vice President, Office of Institutional Equity."[17]

In short, it's a racket, with college administrations pillaging taxpayers, students, and alumni alike, as education bureaucrats get fatter and fatter. Taxpayers are astonished that as their taxes go up, so does in-state tuition for the schools they support. Alumni are shaken down to fund scholarships to pay for the outrageous tuition their alma maters are charging (which also allows the alma maters to brag about how many scholarship students they have). Educational bureaucrats swathe themselves in self-congratulatory language about teaching the next generation—even as they impoverish the next generation. They're confident that no state legislator, no politician, no mass movement wants to be tarred as "anti-education." And with education, they say, surely more is better. You can't spend too many years in a classroom. After all, most professors never left. So why should the students? Needless to say, if you live your life in a classroom—and expect to be financially rewarded for it—it can skew your sense of reality. As philosopher Robert Nozick wrote in his famous essay, "Why Do Intellectuals Oppose Capitalism?":

> It is not surprising, therefore, that [the socialist] distribution of goods and rewards via a centrally organized distributional mechanism later strikes intellectuals as more appropriate than the 'anarchy and chaos' of the marketplace. For distribution in a centrally planned socialist society stands to distribution in a capitalist society as distribution by the teachers stands to distribution by the schoolyard and hallway....
>
> Earlier I said that intellectuals want the society to be the schools writ large. Now we see that the resentment due to a frustrated sense of entitlement stems from the fact that the schools (as a specialized first extra-familial social system) are not the society writ small.[18]

Professors believe there is no life outside the classroom. They get paid for standing up and lecturing to students they regard as inferiors (when they teach at all, rather than just performing abstruse and often worthless "research"). Many of them rail against capitalism (and Christianity, and alleged white racism) while profiting more from capitalist businesses and taxpayers than they could ever earn in any true business occupation. Many of them would have a hard time holding down any sort of real job at all.

Like drug dealers, college administrators want to get you hooked on the opiate of higher education so they can profit further. Given how many kids now go to college—and given how academically subpar college has become—an undergraduate degree is effectively the equivalent of your grandfather's high-school diploma. So, the argument goes, if you are truly ambitious, you clearly need to go further into debt to get a master's degree. If you live in an urban hub full of young, ambitious people, like Washington, D.C., you are sure to have been inundated with advertisements about how an additional master's degree is necessary to advance your career. But, of course, this has its own ratchet effect. If every young striving Capitol Hill employee is working on a master's degree, then you need to go to the next step and get *two* master's degrees—or go to law school.

They've got you addicted.

Of course, "pro-education" politicians happily perpetuate the addiction.

On September 28, 2011, President Barack Obama told high-school students that "Not only do you have to graduate from high school, but you're going to have to continue education after you leave. You have to not only graduate, but you've got to keep going after you graduate.... The fact of the matter is, is that more than 60 percent of the jobs in the next decade will require more than a high school diploma—more than 60 percent. That's the world you're walking into."[19]

In April 2021, President Joe Biden echoed a similar sentiment. A first-grade-through-high-school education, he said, "is no longer enough to compete in the 21st century. That's why the American Families Plan guarantees four additional years of public education for every person in America—two years of the universal, high-quality pre-school and two years of free community college."[20] That's sixteen years of featherbedding for our failed educational establishment. None of us should want that.

In fact, there are four courses of action that could be—and should be—done *now*, if we were truly serious about education.

- First, as preparation: break the current system of K–12 public education that provides little in terms of a real education and merely puts students on a conveyor belt to our clown-college universities. Enact absolute school choice, with no preschool requirements, and insist that parents are the primary educators of their children (which is simply a neglected truth). And if you're a parent, unless you have a stellar private school, home-school your kids. You'll do a better job—you care more about their well-being than anyone else—and you'll have more freedom. The current revolution of parents against radical school boards is a sign that parents are catching on that the trust they placed in our public schools and the people who run them was wildly misplaced—and that the teachers' unions are actually a threat to their children's best interests.
- At the state level, state legislators should slash public funding of state colleges and universities. State funding should be based on how well these schools serve the public interest by requiring courses in the Great Books of Western civilization, American history, and civics; the acquisition of employable skills; and the rate at which

graduates get well-paying private-sector jobs. The state has oversight of these colleges and universities and should use it to make sure that taxpayer dollars are well spent. Texas lieutenant governor Dan Patrick has the right idea in wanting to strictly limit tenure for professors in Texas state colleges and universities and prohibit the teaching of critical race theory as noxious indoctrination that taxpayers shouldn't have to fund.

- At the federal level, the massive taxpayer subsidies and federal funding for research grants need to be overseen more diligently by Congress. Every year we're entertained or horrified at stories of the federal government's wasteful spending on ludicrous "research" at the nation's colleges and universities. It's not just wasteful, it's corrupting, as it puts even allegedly disinterested disciplines—like science—at the mercy of very much interested bureaucrats like Dr. Anthony Fauci, or global-warming bureaucrats, or the rest of the comfortably ensconced and largely unaccountable Washington bureaucracy. This distorts and politicizes science. (That's a big topic; more on that later.) Congressmen need to make oversight of this spending a priority.

- At private schools, alumni need to exert their authority: money talks, as does involvement on alumni boards. Groups like the American Council of Trustees and Alumni are fighting to restore academic standards and accountability to America's colleges and universities.[21] Support them. Join them.

- Still, despite all these efforts, even allegedly conservative politicians have—at least in the past—made *real* education reform a low priority. The successful election of

Governor Glenn Youngkin in Virginia, who ran on a platform of education reform and empowering parents, may be a sign that things are changing. We can hope. But it still seems that few politicians even understand the problem. Democrats and Republicans too often agree that education is simply an unparalleled good—the more the better, *regardless of its content or its cost.* Their failure to act is the reason why we now need a revolution in public education—and a counterrevolution in higher education. And it starts with us, as individuals. Defund the beast! Don't go to college!

But Wait—Aren't the Sciences Worth It?

Okay, but what about the so-called STEM majors in science, technology, engineering, and math? Surely these are a different story. Surely these departments aren't as corrupted by political correctness. Surely here you can learn valuable skills and concepts and facts. Surely here your money could be well spent.

The real answer is maybe—and up to a point.

In his book *Worthless: The Young Person's Indispensable Guide to Choosing the Right Major*, writer Aaron Clarey notes that math has helped keep science and engineering departments sane. "Math is math. It's reality.... Furthermore, the economic REALITY of the situation is that if you want to make a decent living, you have to learn math. There are no ifs, ands, or buts about it. Math is not optional."[22]

Clarey goes on to say that math is meritocratic—that is, "one's mathematical ability is not dependent on some sort of 'aptitude' or 'natural skill.' It's not dependent on your 'gender' or upbringing. It's really more a function of how much effort you've put into it. The reason why is that math is finite. It is logical. It always follows set precise rules. It always has set precise answers…you either got the problem right or you didn't no matter how much the teacher hated you."[23]

Accordingly, if you're determined to go to college, what if you went as a STEM major? In some respects it is certainly the best option, and these departments are the ones most likely to teach you something of value. As one report noted, "The initial starting salary projections for Class of 2019 bachelor's degree graduates strongly indicate that those with STEM degrees will continue to earn the highest starting salaries, according to results of Winter 2019 *Salary Survey*. The top-paid graduates this year are once again expected to earn engineering, computer science, and math and sciences degrees" (with expected salaries of $69,188, $67,539, and $62,177, respectively).[24]

This is not to say that you will be protected from the woke insanity of the modern university. Indeed, Clarey wrote his book in 2011, before the astonishing trajectory of intersectionality had gained its momentum. We had not yet seen university professors, for instance, declare that math is racist, or in the words of one professor, that math is a "harbor for whiteness" and "the very nature of the knowledge and who's produced it, and what has counted as mathematics is itself dominated by whiteness and racism." Or in the words of another professor, "On many levels, mathematics itself operates as whiteness. Who gets credit for doing and developing mathematics, who is capable in mathematics, and who is seen as part of the mathematical community is generally viewed as white."[25]

Oh.

In 2021, the University of Toronto Faculty of Arts and Science, launched its course MAT192H1: "Liberating Mathematics," with the following description:

Currently, mathematics is at a crossroads between tradition and progress. Progress has been led in large part by women mathematicians, in particular Black women, Indigenous women, and women from visible minorities. Intertwined in their studies of mathematics is a daring critique of traditional mathematics, re-imagining of mathematics culture, and more. This course will compare and contrast new forms of accessible mathematics with standard sources that draw dominantly on the experiences and narratives of men.[26]

On her personal blog, "The Liberated Mathematician," (approvingly reposted at the website of the American Mathematical Society) Piper Harron—who was then a temporary assistant professor in Mathematics at the University of Hawaii, Manoa, and is now at the University of Toronto—called on white heterosexual men to "get out [of] the way" and quit their jobs: "If you are a white cis man...you almost certainly should resign from your position of power.... What can universities do? Well, that's easier. Stop hiring white cis men (except as needed to get/retain people who are not white cis men) until the problem goes away.... When you hire a non-marginalized person, you are not just supporting this one applicant whom you like, you are rewarding a person who has been rewarded his whole life. You are justifying the system that makes his application look so good. You are not innocent."[27] Piper Harron, incidentally, prefers the pronouns "they/she" and lists her interests as "intersectional feminism, Number Theory, anti-racism, humanizing mathematics, etc."[28] At Princeton she "survived external and internalized misogyny [and] survived external and internalized racism."[29] Princeton somehow overcame its misogyny and racism enough to grant her a master's degree and Ph.D. in mathematics.

So, it's official: math has gone woke. And it's not just math of course. The American Medical Association, which has a lot of say about what you'll be taught in medical school, has, in the words of reporter John Stossel, "issued a 54-page guide telling doctors things like, don't say 'equality'; say 'equity.' Don't say 'minority'; say 'historically marginalized.' Much of the AMA's advisory sounds like Marxism: 'Expose...property rights...Individualism is problematic...Corporations...limit prospects for good health...[with] people underpaid and forced into poverty as a result of banking policies.'"[30]

And need we go on about Big Tech? It is notoriously woke. As was reported at *Commentary* magazine in an article titled "The Wrath of the Woke Workforce":

> Woke workers at Google...employ similar tactics to those used by "deplatforming" activists on college campuses—the small groups of radical students who engage in loud and disruptive protests in order to convince college administrators to disinvite speakers with whom the radicals disagree (not surprisingly, those speakers are overwhelmingly conservative). This isn't tolerance; it's censorship. And it's unequally applied via a diversity hierarchy where the "wrong" views trump everything else about a person....
>
> Like campus deplatformers, woke workers are on permanent high alert for offenders. As *Wired* described the activities of one trans activist and Google employee, "Over the past few years, she learned to keep a close eye on conversations about diversity issues. It began subtly. Coworkers peppered mailing lists and company town halls with questions: What about meritocracy? Isn't improving diversity lowering the bar? What about viewpoint diversity? Doesn't this exclude white men?" The

employee was quick to report such supposedly intolerant questioning to human resources.[31]

Political correctness is everywhere at your local college and university—including in every STEM field, if not in its actual content, then in the "diversity, equity, and inclusion" mandates that the department will be required to follow. As ridiculous as it sounds (*math is racist!*), this march of stupidity poses a major danger to America's future. The danger includes not only the obvious perils of corrupting the sciences politically (as the humanities have been corrupted) or of affirmative action promoting the less talented (because they check the right intersectionality boxes) over the more talented (not a happy situation if that person is a doctor treating you or an engineer building a bridge), but also the deeper problem of using politicized science to advance a philosophy of "scientism" in its students, and thus in society. Scientism is an ideological ally of Marxism that promotes a reductionist, atheistic, materialist view of man and creation; and it has a very bad history, as we will see.

So, while becoming a STEM major might not be as bad an investment as becoming a humanities major, unless you balance your STEM training with a *real* liberal arts education, as it was traditionally understood, you're likely to be investing in a very skewed view of the world.

We'll conclude this chapter with the classic admonition, *caveat emptor*, buyer beware. Yes, a STEM degree will give you some—but less than you think—protection from university craziness; and it will provide a better economic return on whatever you invest in your college education. But the money isn't the only cost. You don't want to lose your mind—or your soul—by embracing "scientism." That's a much bigger threat than you might know.

CHAPTER FOUR

The Sciences Won't Save You: Why STEM Has Its Limits

"Men became scientific because they expected Law in Nature, and they expected Law in Nature because they believed in a Legislator. In most modern scientists this belief has died: it will be interesting to see how long their confidence in uniformity survives it. Two significant developments have already appeared—the hypothesis of a lawless sub-nature, and the surrender of the claim that science is true. We may be living nearer than we suppose to the end of the Scientific Age."

—C. S. Lewis, *Miracles*

We've seen politicized science many times before—most notoriously in the great tyrannies of the twentieth century. It was Winston Churchill who at the outbreak of the Second World War warned his countrymen:

The whole fury and might of the enemy must very soon be turned on us. Hitler knows that he will have to break us in this Island or lose the war. If we can stand up to him, all Europe may be free and the life of the world may move forward into broad, sunlit uplands. But if we fail, then the whole world, including the United States, including all that we have known and cared for, will sink into the abyss of a new Dark Age made more sinister, and perhaps more pro-tracted, by the lights of perverted science.[1]

The "perverted science" included eugenics, death camps, and all the related horrors of the National Socialist regime in Germany. But the Soviet Union was equally a wielder of perverted science—explicitly politicized science—in ways that attempted to explain away inconvenient facts or theories that seemed to discredit atheistic materialism, in much the same way that the LGBTQ+ mob attempts to discredit biology, psychology, and the plain, unadulterated facts of life. The end results of politicizing science are always and inevitably bad.

The first thing to remember is that materialistic science is not the measure of everything—though scientism makes that claim. As philosopher of science Paul Feyerabend reminds us, "Scientists are salesmen of ideas and gadgets, they are not judges of Truth and Falsehood. Nor are they High Priests of Living."[2]

But it is easy to think they are—especially if you are scientist, or a young science student. Any specialist likes to think that his specialty has more answers than meets the eye, and when it comes to the teaching of science, this is not a harmless conceit. Philosopher Edward Feser notes that Feyerabend believed that "scientists too often made of science a 'tyranny,' claiming rights over the direction of public policy shared by no other interest group in a democratic society. Through the education system, they impose assent to useful but fallible and limited theoretical abstractions as if they were obliga-tory dogmas."[3]

Feyerabend died in 1994, but his observations seem prophetic. We saw a lot of this scientific hubris during the COVID-19 pan-demic, most notoriously with Dr. Anthony Fauci's megalomaniac proclamation that "attacks on me are attacks on science."[4] And we see a lot of scientific cowardice in the university, where supposed upholders of objective scientific truth are quite willing to fudge the definitions of male and female and affirm that men can give birth, if that is what is necessary to keep them in the good graces of those who approve research funding and pay for all their lab assistants, refracting telescopes, Bunsen burners, and Hadron colliders.

The irony perhaps is that their willingness to compromise truth and reality is in part a result of their scientism. As Harvard biologist Richard Lewontin once conceded,

> We take the side of science *in spite* of the patent absurdity of some of its constructs, *in spite* of its failure to fulfill many of its extravagant promises of health and life, *in spite* of the tolerance of the scientific community for unsubstantiated just-so stories, because we have a prior commitment, a commitment to materialism. It's not that the methods and institutions of science somehow compel us to accept a material explanation of the phenomenal world, but on the contrary, that we are forced by our *a priori* adherence to material causes to create an apparatus of investigation and a set of concepts that produce material explanations, no matter how counterintuitive, no matter how mystifying to the uninitiated. Moreover, that Materialism is absolute, for we cannot allow a Divine Foot in the door.[5]

Lewontin admitted that he is "first and foremost a materialist and then a scientist."[6] What he didn't note is that his preference for materialism over science is what makes the practical effect of scientism to be Marxism. And we've witnessed that before in practice in the Soviet Union, which on the basis of "scientific" materialism rejected the big bang theory, quantum mechanics, and Mendelian genetics. The danger of "scientism's" denial of actual science is something that every STEM major should consider. It is an obvious danger with the LGBTQ+ movement, but also with feminism, "anti-racism," and every other form of intersectionality that sees Marxist politics within every aspect of science and even math. We can see where such a politicization of science leads with a quick survey of how the Communist Soviet Union treated these three products of Western science—the big bang theory, quantum mechanics, and Mendelian genetics—that had non-"materialist," as the Marxists regarded it, and thus politically incorrect implications.

Scientism versus the Big Bang

According to the cosmological model known as the big bang theory, the primordial universe was in an extremely high-temperature and compact state that expanded suddenly, then cooled off by stretching out to its present, vast, cooler status. According to this model, the universe continues to expand today.[7]

A Belgian mathematical physicist and Catholic priest named Father Georges Lemaître was the principal formulator of the big bang theory. He insisted that his theory was both scientifically accurate and consistent with his faith. As Duncan Aikman of the *New York Times* wrote in 1933, "There is no conflict between religion and science, the Abbé Lemaître has been telling audiences over and over again in this country.... His view is interesting and important not because he is a Catholic priest, not because he's one of the leading mathematical physicists of our time, but because he is both."[8]

Lemaître described the beginning of the universe "as a burst of fireworks.... He believed this burst of fireworks was the beginning of time, taking place on 'a day without yesterday.'"[9] Lemaître's view of the universe contradicted Albert Einstein's cosmological view (which later came to be known as the "steady state" model and continued to be advanced by other scientists, like astronomer Fred Hoyle),[10] but under mounting evidence, Einstein eventually conceded that Lemaître had been right and that he had been wrong.[11]

Although every scientific theory is just that—a theory—the American Chemical Society considers the big bang theory "the most widely accepted scientific model for the beginning of the universe." Moreover, the big bang theory is "the only scientific theory yet devised that explains the observable features of the universe as we know them today."[12]

Opposition to the big bang theory often came less from scientific reasons than from philosophical ones, because "the Big Bang theory strikes many people as having theological implications."[13] At a November 22, 1951, meeting of the Pontifical Academy of Sciences, Pope Pius XII said that the big bang theory vindicated Catholic teaching that "creation took place. We say: Therefore, there is a Creator. Therefore, God exists!"[14] Anglicans,[15] Lutherans,[16] and Methodists,[17] have also heralded the big bang theory as affirming the Christian doctrine of the universe being a divine creation from nothing. As author Michael Corey writes: "Indeed, creation *ex nihilo* is a fundamental tenet of orthodox Christian theology.... Modern theoretical physicists have also speculated that the universe may have been produced through a sudden quantum appearance 'out of nothing.'" He adds that English physicist "Paul Davies has...claimed that the particular physics involved in the Big Bang *necessitates* creation *ex nihilo*."[18] Davies actually went further and said that "it may seem bizarre, but in my opinion, science [now] offers a surer path to God than religion."[19] In fact, the reverse might be true. If science "necessitates" the longstanding Christian view of spontaneous creation from nothing, it means that science has only tardily affirmed

Christian theology. Indeed, in 1978, NASA scientist Robert Jastrow, "an avowed agnostic," conceded that theologians were "delighted" that astronomical science seemed to support the "biblical view of Genesis."[20]

But not everyone wanted to draw these conclusions. Atheists didn't—and atheistic communists were among the primary philosophical opponents of the big bang theory. This was true even before the big bang theory was fully enunciated. In March 1869, Friedrich Engels wrote to Karl Marx warning him that any idea of a finite universe created from an *ex nihilo* explosion would contradict their atheist beliefs: "Since, according to this theory, in the existing world, more heat must always be converted into other energy than can be obtained by converting other energy into heat, so the original *hot state*, out of which things have cooled, is obviously inexplicable, *even contradictory*, and thus presumes a God."[21] The Soviet Union, which hailed itself as representing "the highest form of atheism,"[22] certainly saw it that way. It committed itself to the view of an eternal, creationless universe. The "Institute of Scientific Atheism of the Academy of Social Sciences under the Central Committee of the Communist Party of the Soviet Union" mandated the "scientific" rejection of all science that it deemed threatening to the Communist Party philosophy of atheism and deterministic materialism.[23]

Writing near the end of the Cold War, Professor Wil van den Bercken noted, "As an ideological monoculture, the Soviet state cannot recognize any alternative or competitive ideologies as being equal in value, whether on political grounds or in the area of *Weltanschauung*. To do so would mean intellectual pluralism and the destruction of the essence of Soviet ideology."[24]

This had huge implications for science. The big bang, relativity theory, many other scientific developments, and even the principle of "entropy seemed opposed to revolution,"[25] and it was the duty of every Soviet citizen to "defend the purity of Marxist-Leninist doctrines in all domains of culture and science."[26]

Andrei Zhdanov, as Second Secretary of the Communist Party, was Communist General Secretary Joseph Stalin's chief ideologue from 1945 to 1948.[27] Science historian Helge Kragh notes that in a speech on June 24, 1947, Zhdanov said, "that Lemaître and his kindred spirits were 'Falsifiers of science [who] want to revive the fairy tale of the origin of the world from nothing.'"[28]

According to Kragh, "Zhdanov's talk marked the beginning of a decade in which cosmology in the sense cultivated by Western physicists and astronomers almost disappeared from Soviet science."[29] Why was cosmology so important? Kragh explains:

> Contrary to sciences such as chemistry, medicine, geology and physics, cosmology has no technological or military applications whatever. In Marxist terminology, it is not a productive force. All the same, because of its traditional association to philosophical and religious world views it has often played a political role, however indirect.... While the new cosmological theories, the Big Bang theory and the rival steady state theory, attracted little political attention in the West—although they did attract some religious attention—in Stalin's Soviet Union cosmology came to be seen as an ideological battleground of great importance.[30]

So, it was no surprise then, that, under Stalin: "Certain cosmological models, in particular of the big bang type, were declared pseudo-scientific and idealistic because they implied a cosmic creation, a concept which was taken to be religious. The result of the ideological pressure was not an independent Soviet cosmology, but that astronomers and physicists abandoned cosmological research in the Western sense. Only in the 1960s did this situation change, and cosmology in the Soviet Union began to flourish.... [This was after a Communist Party-mandated moratorium on cosmology that existed] from about 1947 to 1963."[31]

But when the Soviets faltered in this aspect of their communist faith, the Chinese Communists were prepared to see it through in the 1960s and 1970s:

> While Soviet science was gradually depoliticized during the 1950s and 1960s, the *de facto* ban on cosmology in the Western sense went unchallenged in the People's Republic of China, where radical Maoist ideologues developed their own version of dialectical materialism. The ideological interference with cosmological theory took a new turn during the Cultural Revolution in Mao Zedong's empire, when relativistic cosmology for a period was declared a reactionary and anti-socialist pseudo-science. Fang Lizhi, a physicist who had changed his research interest from solid-state physics to astrophysics, got caught up in the frenzy of the Cultural Revolution.... He was arrested and imprisoned as a class enemy and "rightist," but was able to resume his scientific career. In 1972 he published a theoretical paper in a new physics journal on big bang cosmology and the cosmic microwave radiation, the first of its kind in the People's Republic. Enraged radical Marxists immediately rallied against Fang's heresy and its betrayal of the true spirit of proletarian science. According to one critic, Li Ke, the big bang theory was nothing but "political opium."[32]

Fang Lizhi eventually fled to the United States.

Imagine, though, a future where American universities are awash with Communist Chinese money, where it's "all too easy to find apologists" for the Chinese Communist Party "meddling in American academia," where Chinese Communist Party "operations aimed at mining the West for intellectual property are just one part of China's campus projects." You don't have to imagine that day because it's already here. As Peter Wood of the National Association of Scholars has pointed out, Communist "Chinese influence over American research and American universities has to be reckoned as immense."[33] And it is concentrated in the STEM fields.

Scientism versus Quantum Mechanics

As violently as they rejected big bang cosmology, communists rejected quantum mechanics because it contradicted the Communist Party's belief in "scientific" materialism and determinism. Historian of science Loren R. Graham describes the situation thus:

> The suspicions of the Soviet critics of quantum mechanics and relativity physics were heightened when several prominent West European philosophers and scientists concluded that the probabilistic approach of quantum mechanics meant the end of determinism as a worldview, while the equivalence of matter and energy postulated by relativity theory marked the end of materialism. Several of them concluded that relativity physics and quantum mechanics destroyed the basis of Marxist materialism.[34]

The Soviets enforced Marxist materialism at the penalty of death. On August 21, 1936, for example, Boris Mikhailovich Hessen, a

quantum physicist, was executed by firing squad.[35] At a Soviet conference, Hessen was condemned by name on two separate counts:

> Hessen and his views on physics came under very heavy
> criticism at a conference on the state of Soviet philosophy
> that was held October 17–20, 1930. Although present, he
> was not permitted to speak in his own defense. He was
> denounced as a "metaphysicist of the worst sort," a "pure
> idealist," and as a deserter of the cause of materialism who
> interpreted relativity physics in the same spirit as the
> Western mystic astronomer Arthur Stanley Eddington. He
> was criticized for paying insufficient attention to the ideas
> of Engels and Lenin. Particularly mistaken, said his detrac-
> tors, was his definition of matter as a "synthesis of space
> and time," a wording that came from one of his defenses
> of relativity theory. In the final resolution of the conference
> Hessen was censured by name twice, once for his philo-
> sophical views on relativity theory and again for his opin-
> ions based on quantum mechanics.[36]

Graham records that,

> One of Hessen's bitterest critics was Ernst Kol'man, a
> Czech Marxist who had emigrated to the Soviet Union. In
> an article published in January 1931, Kol'man maintained
> that "wreckers" were trying to corrupt Soviet physics just
> as [so-called] wreckers had earlier tried to disrupt Soviet
> industry. The implication was serious, since the engi-
> neering "wreckers" had been brought to trial and many
> of them imprisoned. Kol'man in the same article tried to

illustrate how the wreckers in physics were trying to discredit materialism:

"'Matter disappears, only equations remain'—this
Leninist description of academic papism in modern physics
gives the clue to the understanding of the wrecker's predi-
lection for the mathematization of every science. The
wreckers do not dare to say directly that they want to
restore capitalism, they have to hide behind a convenient
mask. And there is no more impenetrable mask to hide
behind than a curtain of mathematical abstraction."[37]

Little did the Communist ideologues of the time know that mathematics is "racist," but today's academic activists are just as keen on
ferreting out "academic papism." While they don't yet have the power
to order executions, they certainly have perches to try to deny academic jobs to "white cis men."

Scientism versus Mendelian Genetics

Perhaps the most famous—and deadliest—Soviet pursuit of
scientism was the rejection of Mendelian genetics. The communists
rejected Gregor Mendel's discoveries, which were well established
by science, because he was a Catholic friar and abbot, as well as a
scientist. And what he discovered, again, contradicted communist
ideology.

Working with pea plants, Mendel founded the modern science of
genetics by discovering "the fundamental laws of inheritance." He
"deduced that genes come in pairs and are inherited as distinct units,
one from each parent. Mendel tracked the segregation of parental
genes and their appearance in the offspring as dominant or recessive

traits."[38] Mendel's experiments were conducted in the mid-nineteenth century and gained acceptance in the early twentieth century. But after World War II, Joseph Stalin "'abolished' Mendelian genetics throughout the Soviet Union" as a matter of scientific materialism.[39] He reasoned that Mendel had to be discredited "in Communist thought, because he was a product of the West and of the Church."[40] For the Soviets, it was enough "that Mendel was a priest, [which] was taken as sufficient to discredit his experiments."[41] Of course, it didn't help that Mendel's experiment underlined the importance of biology, inheritance, and family under a Soviet regime dedicated to egalitarianism, classism, and statism.

Instead of Mendel, the Soviets promoted the theories of their own politically correct botanist Trofim Lysenko.[42] Stalin's enforcement of Lysenkoism as Soviet "scientific" doctrine "crippled Soviet biology for decades."[43] And, as was the Soviet way, executions followed.

> Since the CPSU [Communist Party of the Soviet Union] was so keen to identify its type of atheism as the essential component of the "scientific, materialist *weltanschauung*," problems tended to arise when scientific theories seemed to be in disagreement with the ideological positions of the party. One common consequence, at least during the Stalinist period, was simply to deny that the problematic sciences were true sciences. The most notorious episode was the banning for nearly two decades of the study and research of Mendelian Genetics (incidentally, founded by a Catholic monk). During this period, hundreds of scientists were imprisoned or killed, the most prominent being Nikolai Vavilov, who was starved to death in the Gulag in 1943. (A striking contrast with Galileo, who died in his bed.)[44]

As geneticist Anna C. Pai has written, under Stalin's directive "an entire area of science was suppressed for 20 years. Vavilov and other geneticists were arrested, imprisoned, and finally perished. All existing genetic experimentation was destroyed, and references to Mendel and Darwin were removed."[45]

But it wasn't just scientists who suffered. Lysenko's crackpot theories led to catastrophic famines in the Soviet Union and Communist China. As journalist Sam Kean noted in *The Atlantic*, "Although it's impossible to say for sure, Trofim Lysenko probably killed more human beings than any individual scientist in history. Other dubious scientific achievements have cut thousands upon thousands of lives short: dynamite, poison gas, atomic bombs. But Lysenko, a Soviet biologist, condemned perhaps millions of people to starvation through bogus agricultural research—and did so without hesitation."[46]

So, you get the idea. The same neo-Marxists who corrupted the humanities are just as eager to corrupt the sciences. If they succeed in doing so, the results could be catastrophic. If you go to college and become a STEM major, be on your guard: the woke mob is coming for you too.

CHAPTER FIVE

Adult Day Care:
Why College Will Retard Your Maturity

"I misjudged you ... you're not a moron. You're only a case of arrested development."

—Ernest Hemingway, *The Sun Also Rises*

Idealistic parents and high-school students might still assume that college is a place to grow up, mature, and "find yourself." Unfortunately, today's college campus deliberately infantilizes matriculants. It provides "safe spaces,"[1] works to avoid "triggering" students, and offers risibly childish consolation prizes such as coloring books, kitty-cats, and puppies to help students "cope" with the alleged stress of college living.[2] It's really a form of adult daycare, though in real daycare the children eventually grow up. In the college version, immaturity and egoistic gratification is encouraged as a lifestyle.

Real maturity comes with getting married and having children. But guess what happens when you delay those markers of a mature life for college, paying off college debt, maybe acquiring a graduate degree, and pursuing a career "plan"? It often leads to people *not* getting married—and *not* sacrificing for someone else, and *not* supporting a family—until their thirties, if they ever do.

It didn't used to be this way, of course. It used to be taken for granted that young men needed to go out to work and earn a living to support a family. It used to be assumed that young women would want to get married and raise a family. Those, we're now told, were the bad old days of patriarchy. But in fact, most women *do* want to get married and become mothers (no matter how hard college tries to teach them that marriage and motherhood are "settling" for *less* than a career); and most men, to have any sense of self-worth and self-respect, yearn to excel at a job and to be a married father rather than a fornicator (no matter how hard college encourages them to pursue idle studies and delay marriage). That's what most people want, but instead, thanks to college and college-influenced culture, they've been sold a bill of goods that distracts from that goal—and that in some cases prevents them from achieving it. They are told they need to extend what de facto become their preadult years in pursuit of a degree (or degrees) and career over marriage. The career easily becomes all about "me," and it's only after the fact, sadly, that too many women realize that they have deferred marriage and children too long and too many men realize that they have truly failed to grow up and mature and fulfill their manhood as responsible fathers and providers.

This is one of life's plain truths. It is one of many such plain truths that our education system has chosen to obfuscate and deny and repudiate. That can only have unhappy consequences. It also entails a denial of biology. Women are egg-bearers, and it is shocking (at least to college kids) to learn that the average female will have lost—forever—more than *60 percent* of her eggs by the age of twenty. By age thirty-two, she will have permanently lost more than *85 percent* of her eggs.[3] Consider, too, that those remaining eggs are not of the same high quality as her younger years' eggs: "Because women are born with all the eggs they will ever have, egg quality also deteriorates with aging. Egg quality refers mainly to the genetic makeup of the egg. As women age, the machinery that each egg is equipped with to ensure it maintains the right amount of genetic material, or DNA, can break down over time."[4] In short, while baby boomers (and every indoctrinated generation since then) might think "don't marry young" is good advice, the biological facts of human life beg to differ. If we actually listened to what our bodies—and souls—were telling us, we'd know that our life's purpose lies in marriage and family, and that we were wired to get married young.

No less an authority than Aristotle stated: "And what could be more divine than this, or more desired by a man of sound mind, than to beget by a noble and honored wife children who shall be the most loyal supporters and discreet guardians of their parents in old age, and the preservers of the whole house? Rightly reared by father and mother, children will grow up virtuous, as those who treated them piously and righteously deserve that they should."[5] But what Aristotle calls "divine" is something that college supporters say should be deferred—perhaps forever.

So mass-manufactured collegians have given us a society where young graduates join the work force and run around cities and suburbs thinking like self-obsessed adolescents, yet aping many of the purposive movements of busy grown-ups who head families. It's become a cliché to hear a father remark of his twenty-nine-year-old son: "That kid can do anything he wants to, when he's ready." Bear this in mind: that "kid" is just a few years shy of middle age, and his father is already a senior citizen.

"Arrested development" has fallen out of use among psychologists,[6] perhaps because too many of their patients suffer from it. In popular media, it has been replaced with the idea of "adulting," which is simply a way of repackaging something bad to make it seem inconsequential, or even good. In 2016 Katy Steinmetz of *Time* magazine had this to say in an article titled "This is What 'Adulting' Means":

According to Jane Solomon...a big factor is millennials and their "delayed development" (which isn't necessarily as unfortunate as it sounds).

"This generation of millennials," she says, "they go through life stages that other generations have gone through much later in life, like starting families, owning homes. Maybe they won't own homes at all." The age of first-time mothers is indeed at a historic high of 26. Real-estate site Zillow found that first-time home-buyers are more likely to be older and single today than in past decades. We've all heard about millennials' boomeranging....

Depending on the person and their listeners, different motivations may be driving the "adulting" utterance. It may be the speaker's insecurity at so rarely finding themselves in an adult posture well into their 30s. . . .

While some find the phrase cute and cuddly, others do not. Jezebel writer Madeleine Davies believes there is a "self-congratulatory" vein to this, an expectation of millennials to be applauded for "fulfilling your basic responsibilities as a human," which she finds to be "pretty much the most childish thing imaginable."[7]

Madeleine Davies has it right: "adulting" is ridiculously "self-congratulatory" and "the most childish thing imaginable." There is nothing to be admired in a generation that perpetuates its own sense of adolescence, delays adulthood, and even "boomerangs" back to live with its parents. Falling American birth rates—which have been below replacement rate "generally" since 1971 and "consistently" since 2007, hitting a record low in 2020[8]—are not a sign of a society that is rightly ordered, happy, or healthy.

The Thirty-One Flavors of Arrested Development

Marrying your high-school sweetheart used to be thing. A commonly understood thing. A commonly practiced thing. But you will find that couples rarely form in high school anymore. Guidance counselors can tell you the reason: kids see no point in getting boyfriends or girlfriends because they'll be leaving eventually for college. And parents enthusiastically support this. Moms and dads alike want their kids to "grow up" and "gain experience," not realizing that the experience their kids will gain will not be morally formative (which will likely mean foregoing grandkids) and that they are actually discouraging their kids from growing up.

Aristotle teaches that "virtue is not an act but a habit,"[9] and one of the degrading aspects of delaying adulthood is that it delays the habits of virtue and encourages the habits of vice; it delays the acceptance of responsibility and self-sacrifice; it encourages callowness and selfishness. While unmarried young men busy themselves accumulating life experience (of a very shallow and typically immoral sort), college experience, work experience, travel experience, and a manifold of consensual but noncommittal paramours, they are gathering corresponding habits that will impair their attempt (if it is ever made) to reach real adulthood, manhood, and fatherhood.

To compound this *moral* fact is a *logistical* one. The coeducational settings of late high school and early college provide easily the most natural, facile environment for meeting and mingling with the opposite sex. The workplace does not. The after-work "happy hours" frequented by young, urban professionals do not. Both come with all sorts of complications. Meeting a spouse only becomes harder after high school or college, which is one huge reason why online dating has become a thing for those who have delayed adulthood. If fewer people went to college, more people would put more emphasis on their social life in high school—and in a healthy way, the healthy way that made a previous generation so nostalgic for the 1950s. (It's also one reason leftists hate that era.)

Why "Home Ec" Makes More Sense than University Feminism

Another reason leftists hate the 1950s—and the past in general—is because that era better recognized the way human education should be ordered. Education is meant to be preparation for a virtuous human life, and it includes practical training in the home economy, or what in the 1950s was called "home ec" for short. The Greek word for home economy is *oikonomia*, which means "household management" and stood for *economics*, properly understood.

Economics centers upon efficiency, and for thousands upon thousands of years—up until three generations ago—men and women learned and filled categorically disparate household roles. Getting away from that understanding hasn't been a matter of progress. Back in the bad old days of "gendered" education, young men had wood-shop and mechanics and home-repair courses, and young women learned about how to manage a home. In short, that education *assumed* that high-school boys and girls would be getting married and that knowing how to balance a checkbook and how to run a traditional, patriarchal household was a good and necessary thing. University feminism (and the present university system, more broadly) "killed" home economics.[10] In its place we have a new assumption: that marriage and family are to be deferred, that people will more likely live alone, and that college and career take precedence over homelife. We take this new settlement for granted, but we shouldn't. Sending more kids to college, prying women from the home and shaming them into the workplace, requiring college credentials for jobs that don't actually need them (and for which college provides no skills anyway)—none of these things is making us a happier, healthier, or more virtuous society. In fact, the reverse is true: these things are demonstrably making us unhappier, less healthy (fatter, less virile, less fecund, more drug-dependent), less self-sufficient in practical adult tasks, and with fragile or non-forming families. But then again, maybe that's the point.

In 1975, wizened French feminist Simone de Beauvoir told American feminist Betty Friedan: "No woman should be authorized to stay at home to raise her children. Society should be totally different. Women should not have that choice [to stay at home], precisely because if there is such a choice, too many women will make that one. It is a way of forcing women in a certain direction."[11] According to a 2013 Pew Research Center report, more than 70 percent of mothers with grade-school children work outside the home, even though only 16 percent of adults "say the ideal situation for a young child is to have a mother who works full time."[12] So we have sacrificed homelife and the best interests of children in favor of women pursuing careers.

And how has that turned out? Actually, not so well. In *The Paradox of Declining Female Happiness*,[13] economists Betsey Stevenson and Justin Wolfers "analyzed the happiness trends of US citizens between 1970 and 2005 and found a surprising result. Stevenson and Wolfers discovered that American women rated their overall life satisfaction higher than men in the 1970s. Thereafter, women's happiness scores decreased while men's scores stayed roughly stable. By the 1990s, women were less happy than men."[14]

Home economics courses started getting phased out in the 1970s. Often they were replaced in high school by college preparation courses. And now *colleges* are having to teach their own ideologically repurposed version of home economics. As Fox Business reports:

Many students entering college haven't mastered basic life skills such as changing a tire or balancing a checkbook, so some universities are responding with noncredit workshops sometimes called "Adulting 101."...

While older generations might scoff at millennials and Generation Z for not knowing how to perform these tasks, educators say today's college students grew up under intense pressure to pass college entrance exams and achieve high grade point averages—giving them little time to learn life skills. Hovering parents and a decline in traditional home economics classes also contributed to the problem.

When high schools began focusing on core subjects for testing, classes known as home economics or family and consumer science began to decline. By 2012, fewer than 3.5 million students were taking such classes, a 38% drop in a decade.

"It's not considered to be a core area, and so it's easier to say, 'maybe we don't need this,'" said Duane Whitbeck, the chair of Family and Consumer Sciences at Pittsburg State University.

Students working with Kansas State's health center organized workshops because they had few opportunities to learn life skills.

"We don't have classes on how to change a tire at school," said student Frankie Skinner. "We lack knowledge of just basic adulting."[15]

These new adulting courses aren't, of course, about how to manage a household as husband and wife, but rather how to live single, alone, and childless as a student-debt-burdened, smart-city professional—or maybe, at best, in a "genderless" two-income household where there is no traditional division of labor. Yet, before she became a woke United States senator, even Elizabeth Warren acknowledged that an economy that required two-income households was not a socially desirable one. In her 2003 book *The Two Income Trap: Why Middle-Class Mothers and Fathers Are Going Broke* (coauthored with her daughter), Warren argues that two-income families are actually getting poorer and putting themselves at greater risk of bankruptcy than the previous generation's single-income families because of a rapidly increased cost of living, while also stating that stay-at-home mothers are "the most important part of the safety net" of society.[16]

In truth, the spike in the cost of living is largely driven by the economic assumptions of a two-income, everyone-goes-to-college, household model. Those economic assumptions include the need for daycare, the search for real estate in good school districts, college tuitions, and so on. It is a college- and feminist-inspired vicious economic circle. The way to break that circle is to go back to a better social model. Most of us shouldn't go to college, shouldn't have that crippling student debt, shouldn't have that deadly delay of adulthood, shouldn't suffer that four—or more—years of neo-Marxist indoctrination. Instead, young people should be encouraged to marry young and establish one-income households. *This is the heart of the revolution, or counterrevolution, that will restore American society.*

Instead of paying for daycare—which "now costs as much as buying a brand new Hyundai Elantra each year,"[17] according to *The Atlantic*—how about having mothers taking on that role, as their children would certainly prefer? Instead of mothers abandoning their homes, what about mothers abandoning the workplace and demanding that their husbands be good, responsible providers? Instead of delaying the formation of families and making women and children unhappier and men more immature and less marriageable, what about doing what works? That would give us a better society—one that wouldn't need "adulting" courses.

Trades, Tools, and Work by Hands

Another thing that would help make our society better is for more young men to skip college and go to work—and not just any work, but working with their hands. It is a myth propagated by the college huckster that we need more college graduates. As Sarah Chamberlain noted in *Forbes*: "America is facing an unprecedented skilled labor shortage.... Our country is suffering because of it.... Roads, highways, bridges, locks, dams, harbors, water systems, and airports have been neglected or only marginally repaired in the last twenty years." A big part of the problem, she notes is "our culture's emphasis on going to college." She continues:

> Many high schools look to their university placement as the best judge of a quality education. That statistic discriminates against students for whom college is just not a good fit, especially when schools do little to inform students of non-collegiate options. It is unfortunate for those students who try college, but eventually drop out, feeling like a failure, when in fact, it wasn't the right place for them from the start.
>
> Recognizing high tuition costs, long term student loan debt, and difficulties finding a job in the field of their college major should be motivating young men and women to look at better paying alternatives from the onset. Many are already skilled at working with their hands, and prefer jobs where they can move around rather than sitting at a desk all day. High school career counselors would be doing students a big

favor by informing them about the benefits of getting into technical trades. Parents who best understand their son or daughter's interests may also do well to encourage career options aside from immediately attending college. It's time we reduce the stigma around technical training. Skilled labor is not a fallback position, but a genuine positive career choice.[18]

What we really need are not more college graduates, but more construction workers, builders, men with skilled trades, men to work as electricians and pipefitters, truck drivers and oil riggers, men who use their hands as tools. In the wake of the coronavirus pandemic, it became clear that America needs to bring manufacturing back to this country; and it was equally clear, even before the pandemic, that we have a gaping labor shortage in skilled blue-collar workers.

TV show host Mike Rowe has become a celebrity spokesman for the American blue-collar worker. He says, quite rightly, in our opinion, that "people with dirty jobs are happier than you think. As a group, they're the happiest people I know,"[19] which makes sense, because man was made to work with his hands. Building something, crafting something, solving a mechanical problem provides an innate sense of satisfaction.[20]

He goes on: "We're churning out a generation of poorly educated people with no skill, no ambition, no guidance, and no realistic expectations of what it means to go to work."[21] True, to which we would add, it's a generation of no smarts, no morals, no guts, and no ability build or fix things, but with an insufferable lack of Socratic humility and an equally insufferable pomposity about being well-educated when they're not.

Rowe continues: "Happiness does not come from a job. It comes from knowing what you truly value, and behaving in a way that's consistent with those beliefs."[22] This is spot-on: no job will, by itself, render a human being happy. But the happiest are those men and women who marry young, work hard, have large families, and on nights and weekends educate themselves with true sources of wisdom. They aren't *careerists* or *degree-chasers*, they are men and women doing what they were made to do.

Rowe understands that "we're lending money we don't have to kids who can't pay it back to train them for jobs that no longer exist. That's nuts." And the nub of the issue is this: "The flaw in our character is our insistence on separating blue-collar jobs from white-collar jobs, and encouraging one form of education over another."[23] Yes, computers, algorithms, and the management of abstract symbols in one's head can be part of an education—and even necessary for the engineers we need—but also necessary is the ability to roll up one's sleeves, get one's hands dirty, and actually build or fix something for oneself. Indeed, as Will Knowland, a former teacher at Eton Academy and an amateur powerlifter, notes, "Be suspicious of people who don't lift or do heavy labour. It teaches valuable lessons. Heavy isn't a social construct. You don't get gains you don't earn. And if you 'identify' as strong, it doesn't make it true."[24] Bottom line, education needs to get back not only to hard academic subjects but to home economics for young women and the trades for young men. That's what will bring our society moral contentment.

Hook-Up U

In addition to the woke ideological indoctrination and the stunting effects on adulthood, there is another reason—one rarely talked about—for young Americans not to go to college: *sexual degeneracy*. Sexual degeneracy is not only often officially promoted on college campuses but (unfortunately) also largely ignored by parents who either just don't want to know, or feel compromised themselves, or think it is inevitably (and not wrongly) part of a college experience. For these latter parents, it is a normalized rite of passage for millions of young men and women to go to college for four years with the expectation that students will repeatedly get blackout drunk and have meaningless, transactional sex. Our society as a whole seems unconcerned about how this might alter the moral outlook of generation after generation, not just in terms (at a minimum) of legitimized fornication, promiscuity, and sterility, but also in terms of normative sexual boundaries and definitions of deviancy (as with the LGBTQ+ movement, which is stronger on campus than anywhere else).

Let us be clear, we are *not* saying that our analysis here applies equally to *all* colleges and universities or to *every* student's particular experience. What we are saying is that the data—statistical and anecdotal—suggests this is what the culture is like at a *majority* of college and university campuses. As with STEM majors, if you must go college, think very carefully about the culture in which you will study and live. Examples of university-sponsored degeneracy could fill a book. Moreover, it has been going on for decades. But it still has the capacity to shock with its uninhibited insanity. For instance, as was reported in the opinion/letters section of the *Wall Street Journal*, Harvard's 2016 "Sex Week" kicked off its festivities in Harvard's Holden Chapel with "'a film screening + a massive raffle of sex toys, safer-sex supplies, and other such joys.'" Meanwhile, "other events included Feminist Porn; Feeling Myself: Conversations About Masturbation; Sex Letter Writing; Sex Toys; and The Guide to BDSM in the College Dorm Room. The latter event featured, 'cool demonstrations with whips, floggers, and more!'"[25]

This is to not be confused with Harvard's official student-led porn club,[26] or Bondage, Domination, and Sado-Masochism club,[27] or student-led porn magazine, "H Bomb," which itself is not to be confused with Vassar College's student-led porn magazine, "Squirm."

College Magazine highlights that Columbia University:

> Offers a sexual health map showing locations around campus where you can find safe sex supplies like male and female condoms, dental dams, lubricant, and a safer sex brochure. As one female student noted, "In my opinion, Columbia is a very forward-thinking and open-minded community. Hooking up at many schools can be incredibly demeaning and degrading for women, but at Columbia I think it's very different. We are a lot more progressive than other schools. We preach equality."[28]

Columbia might think it is more "progressive," but as the magazine points out, many other schools take similar attitudes. For instance, Oregon State University offers room assignments based on "gender identity" and there are "condom hotspots located all over campus that are basically boxes that have condoms, lube, female condoms, finger condoms, really all kinds of stuff, and it is all free." The University of Oregon, similarly, offers "free birth control, emergency contraception, HIV testing, free condoms, lube and pregnancy testing." The University of Georgia has the "Condom Express," that "delivers free condoms to dorms on campus." The university also held a "Project Condom Fashion Show." The University of Michigan at Ann Arbor has "free condoms and safe sex items available at the Wellness Center." The University of Connecticut has "Sexual goodie bags [with] 12 condoms, dental dams and lube."[29] The examples really are endless—and these came from an article *praising* college hook-up culture.

Of course, concomitant with degeneracy on campus—as in society at large—are declining rates not only of marriage and motherhood and fatherhood, but declining rates of sexual activity overall.[30]

Sex really does belong, exclusively, in marriage, it turns out. As Rudyard Kipling told us in his brilliant poem "The Gods of the Copybook Headings":

> *On the first Feminian Sandstones we were promised the Fuller Life*
> *(Which started by loving our neighbour and ended by loving his wife)*
> *Till our women had no more children and the men lost reason and faith,*
> *And the Gods of the Copybook Headings said: "The Wages of Sin is Death."*[31]

The debauched campus culture is formed and reinforced by alleged scholarship and endless courses that promote the LGBTQ+ agenda, under which, by definition, anything goes. A lesson of history that seems to be necessary to learn over and over again is that a sexually depraved society inevitably leads to a lonely and barren wasteland aching to be overrun by foreign invaders (or immigrants to make up for population shortfalls). That outcome seems to be another "progressive" goal.

Sexual degeneracy on campus runs along a parallel track with concerns about sexual violence and byzantine guidelines on "consent." Antioch College's sexual-offense protocols and guidelines have set the standard. Adopted in 1991 at the prompting of the so-called "Womyn of Antioch," the consent requirements made national attention—and were mocked—at the time because of their ridiculous step-by-step demands for consent and pretense of legalism.[32] Nevertheless, as of 2014, more than eight hundred colleges had jumped on board with the so-called "affirmative consent" movement, pledging to adopt student sexual protocols on the Antioch model,[33] which only goes to show

how swiftly the ridiculous becomes the required at our colleges and universities.

Things were much easier—and saner—when the norm was the Christian one, that sex outside of marriage is wrong, colleges acted in *loco parentis* to discourage fornication (including with single-sex dorms), and people got married and took on adult responsibilities when they were young. In lieu of that, we have the radical battering down of nearly all traditional norms with respect to what counts as sex, rape, flirting, sexual harassment, courtships, relationships, exclusivity, abuse, consent, and an entirely new set of ambiguous, contradictory, and constantly evolving ad hoc norms that have resulted in confusion in identifying and quantifying sexual assaults on campus. As journalist Alia Wong reported in *The Atlantic*, "The problem is that every statistic about campus sexual assault seems to be contradicted or challenged by another one."[34] Ever-changing definitions is part of the problem.

Things were better when we had a grown-up culture. A culture that knew something about history and the facts of life. In his famous book *Sex and Culture*, sociologist J. D. Unwin found that cultures and civilizations rise when they practice what we would now call old-fashioned sexual virtue and monogamy and decline when they do not.[35] Unwin's findings were echoed by Sir John Glubb in his essay, "The Fate of Empires and the Search for Survival." Glubb noted that nations generally rose and fell over the course of a 250-year arc, covering six "ages," the Age of Pioneers, the Age of Conquests, the Age of Commerce, the Age of Affluence, the Age of Intellect, and the Age of Decadence. Regarding the Age of Decadence, Glubb writes of medieval Baghdad:

> The contemporary historians of Baghdad in the early tenth century.... deplored the degeneracy of the times in which

they lived, emphasizing particularly the indifference to religion, the increasing materialism and the laxity of sexual morals....

The historians commented bitterly on the extraordinary influence acquired by popular singers over young people, resulting in a decline in sexual morality. The "pop" singers of Baghdad accompanied their erotic songs on the lute, an instrument resembling the modern guitar.... Several khalifs issued orders banning "pop" singers from the capital, but within a few years they always returned....

Many women practised law, while others obtained posts as university professors. There was an agitation for the appointment of female judges, which, however, does not appear to have succeeded.

Soon after this period, government and public order collapsed, and foreign invaders overran the country.[36]

It would seem clear that by Glubb's standards we are in an age of decadence.

Decadence comes from not working to uphold civilization, from not seeing life as a quick march to maturity and duty, from men and women not recognizing that their most important role in life is to take on the fundamental, specific responsibilities of being a providing father and a nurturing mother.

CHAPTER SIX

What a University Should Be
(and Where It's Going)

"A nation is born stoic, and dies epicurean. At its cradle (to repeat a thoughtful adage) religion stands, and philosophy accompanies it to the grave. In the beginning of all cultures a strong religious faith conceals and softens the nature of things, and gives men courage to bear pain and hardship patiently; at every step the gods are with them, and will not let them perish, until they do. Even then a firm faith will explain that it was the sins of the people that turned their gods to an avenging wrath; evil does not destroy faith, but strengthens it. If victory comes, if war is forgotten in security and peace, then wealth grows; the life of the body gives way, in the dominant classes, to the life of the senses and the mind; toil and suffering are replaced by pleasure and ease; science weakens faith even while thought and comfort weaken virility and fortitude. At last men begin to doubt the gods; they mourn the tragedy of knowledge, and seek refuge in every passing delight. Achilles is at the beginning, Epicurus at the end. After David comes Job, and after Job, Ecclesiastes."

—Will Durant, *Our Oriental Heritage*

Karl Marx famously critiqued the goal of philosophers to the extent that they "have tried to understand the world in various ways; the point, however, is not to understand it but rather to *change it*."[1] On his own terms, Marx succeeded: he drastically changed the world in ways reflective of no understanding at all. Our colleges and universities have essentially taken up that same banner. "We all want to change the world," is an old lyric and an old story; and it has led our colleges and universities in the direction of insanity—and likely an even-more-frightening future, as we'll see. It has led to a denial of reality, of understanding the world as it is, of recognizing that the order of the world has meaning (all the way down to the order of two biological sexes). None of this is an accident. All of this explains why we refer to the dominant forces in higher education as neo-Marxist. Those who run our universities do not want to understand the world, they want to change it. And by funneling millions of students into college classrooms, we aid the neo-Marxists, and so do the liberal faculty members who have proven morally incapable of stopping them. As a wise man once said: "Communists are just liberals who know what they're doing."

Changing the world is the reverse of the universities' proper purpose, which is to understand the world. The old philosophers were right, which is why, if we are to achieve the counterrevolution we need in higher education, their philosophy, a better philosophy, will need to be restored to the center of a core curriculum.

The point of philosophy—and of all academic disciplines—should be to understand the world and what is real. And that means going back to philosophical first principles and restoring the "perennial philosophy" of Aristotle and Saint Thomas Aquinas to pride of place at the university and organizing academic disciplines around it.

As the New World Encyclopedia puts it, Thomism (the philosophy of Saint Thomas Aquinas) "synthesized the principles of Aristotle with the doctrines of the Christian faith.... The ensuing school of thought became one of the most influential philosophies of all time."[2] It was the philosophy at the core of the entire idea of the university when it was created by the Catholic Church in the Middle Ages. It remained the foundation stone of a proper education long thereafter, surviving attacks on it from the time of the Reformation through the Enlightenment and beyond. These anti-Thomistic reductionist, materialist, determinist, subjectivist theories slowly eroded what had been the entire Western basis of knowledge, undermining the ideas of objective truth, natural law, and moral order.

In American colleges and universities, the Aristotelian-Thomistic philosophical tradition—though rarely explicitly enunciated outside of Catholic schools—provided a sort of intellectual backdrop for the old "core curriculum" that was a major part of every undergraduate's experience and was meant to expose freshmen and sophomores to the Great Books, the essential ideas of Western civilization, and the foundations of America's "civic religion" in the Declaration of Independence, the *Federalist Papers*, and the Constitution.

But the single biggest fix for all that ails our colleges and universities would be to recenter them on the perennial philosophy of Aristotle and Saint Thomas Aquinas and that philosophy's view of "natural law." Natural law itself can be defined as a "system of right or justice held to be common to all humans and derived from nature rather than from the rules of society, or positive law."[3]

Thomistic natural law can be easily explained as having three prongs.

First, natural law dictates that man is a uniquely rational animal, and for him nature is a place of moral freedom. Man, unlike other animals, bears *free will* to make moral decisions. Free will is controversial because it is a Catholic idea, largely denied by Reformation Protestants and by the materialist and determinist philosophers who arose during the Enlightenment and after. But if we are to restore sanity to academic life and teaching, we need to affirm that man is a rational animal capable of making free-will moral decisions.

Second, natural law dictates that for man, nature is intelligible. Man can learn from and about his surroundings. To say the obvious, this prong is necessary to true science. But this prong, too, is controversial—historically because Reformation Protestants held that only scripture is fully and theologically intelligible. Enlightenment philosophers and their successors have cast doubt that "knowledge" can consist of anything other than sensory impressions. That's one of the ways that secular philosophy undermines true science and that Catholic philosophy supports true science. If we want true science to flourish in our academies, we need to recover this understanding.

Third, nature is teleological. That is, nature has a purpose and a goal. Materialists and determinists reject this, believing that nature is an accident. Thomistic natural law sees nature as created with meaning. That of course is part and parcel of Saint Thomas Aquinas's belief that natural law is "nothing else than the participation of the eternal law [of God] in the rational creature" that is man.[4] In short, it is the objective truth, to which all human knowledge should be striving.

If your idea of college is reading the great works of the Western canon, debating to find the great truths (as in the Socratic method seen in the dialogues of Plato), living a life dedicated to moral and intellectual development (the goal of all properly ordered education), then you have a Thomistic view of a university—and you will find very few schools that share your goals. They might present themselves as such. They know that this image is an attractive one. But they are about something else altogether, with very different ideas of what constitutes moral and intellectual development.

All individuals and institutions operate on the basis of a philosophy, whether consciously held or simply unconsciously assumed.

That philosophy may be ill-expressed. It may be inconsistent. It may even be incoherent. But it is there—and today, in the university, the only two viable philosophical contenders to direct and guide higher education are neo-Marxism and Thomism.

Neo-Marxism is regnant now with all the negative results we have seen. It is somewhat incoherent in itself, but that is a feature, not a bug. The feature is to advance *changing the world*, which, in more accurate terms, means undoing our Christian, Thomistic understanding of the world, and to that end coherence is less important than simply undoing Christian civilization with whatever tool is at hand. As I (Michael) point out in my farewell to the academic life, the contradictory opinions of campus "liberals" and neo-Marxists, are laughable:

Western science is an oppressive structure of the white-male patriarchy that we are dutybound to oppose and deconstruct, but we must trust the latest COVID-19 biomedical data. We must trust the latest COVID-19 biomedical data, but the biomedical categories of male and female are just social constructs. The categories of male and female are just social constructs that can be chosen at will, but the category of race cannot be similarly chosen at will because race is ostensibly an objective natural kind. But race is also just a social construct. But neither of these previous claims is true since race doesn't refer to anything at all because there is only one race, the human race. But whites oppress blacks. Objective evolutionary data discredits God and objective morality, but that same evolutionary data as it relates to heritable features due to race is suddenly just a social construct again. We are in a radically relativistic, post-truth world, but we must guard against conservative fake news. There is no historical meta-narrative, but the events of slavery and colonialism are undeniable objective facts. The patriarchy of Christianity is bad, but the patriarchy of Islam, of the very same Abrahamic tradition, is to be lauded and venerated. Obesity is a social construct but also a marker of objective health at any weight. Atheist-materialist science proves that life is fundamentally meaningless and worthless, but for heaven's sake, will someone please think of the rights, dignity, and intrinsic value of animals and future generations threatened by climate change. A priori mathematics and logic are just socially constructed systems of oppression. There is no such thing as objective truth, but CNN reports just the facts. And what do we even mean by "truth" anyway? And so on. The amount of mental gymnastics required for these folks to simultaneously hold such blatant and obvious contradictions all while walking, talking, and even sometimes operating heavy machinery is truly a sight to behold, impressive as it is horrifying.[5]

It might be obvious, then, that while Thomism is meant to advance actual *knowledge*, neo-Marxism is meant to advance *propaganda*, which is true to Marx's goal of putting change (revolution) above understanding (wisdom). The overwhelming majority of college-educated Americans enter and leave college without ever understanding this basic point. Their alma maters are devoted to propagandizing students and implanting within them (without their even knowing it) neo-Marxist assumptions.

Even when college graduates or their parents do figure this out or acknowledge it, it only strengthens their pacifying belief that "the kids will grow out of it." Once they're in the "real world," then reality will reassert itself, the reality of dollars and cents, of making a living, of getting married and having children. Only that doesn't work when the corporations have gone woke, when government has gone woke, when the institutions have gone woke, and the culture is encouraging neo-Marxist wokeness always and everywhere, even down to television advertisements.

Reality doesn't assert itself—at least not in the way parents hope it will. Their children don't get married (or get married very late) and don't have kids (but support animal adoption). They don't have children themselves, because the wife's too old or it's bad for the environment (or something), but somehow the environment is improved by bringing in millions of immigrants who will keep the economy going and make up for population shortfalls. That sort of "logic" is another reason why the neo-Marxists are winning—because parents and kids don't realize how they're being duped, led astray, and brainwashed. Our college-educated classes have little self-awareness. By any objective historical measure, they're immature, childish, and paranoid (as the COVID-19 pandemic highlighted), but they think they're smart—that's one of their chief conceits—and better than past generations (about whom they know little or nothing, which is why they denigrate them). Thomism provides a road back to sanity—and to a much deeper and truer understanding of what it means to be human.

And that points out an even bigger problem. What it means to be "human" is one of the many things that the neo-Marxists of higher education are aiming to change.

The Perils and Bankruptcy of Transhumanism

It might sound like dystopian science fiction, but it's easy to forget that to our grandparents a lot of what we've been living through now is dystopian science fiction. Homosexual "marriage" and single-sex "parents" are something they never expected to see; nor did they ever expect to hear arguments over invented pronouns ("What?") or

about something called transgenderism ("What the heck is that?").
It's easy to forget that these are things never before seen in history—
and they don't represent progress; they represent something much
more sinister. Transgenderism has itself become a bizarre stepping-
stone for redefining what it means to be human (not just male or
female). It has been adopted by the general ideology of scientism, in
an apparently odd pairing of rationalist determinism and postmodern
wokeism, to advance into *transhumanism*. But what seems an odd
pairing actually isn't. Scientism and wokeism often walk hand in
hand. Their common goal is to *change the world* rather than understand it. Or really, *to change mankind*.

It is not a new idea. Changing mankind has, for instance, been
the point of every communist revolution, each dedicated to remaking
human nature and making a better communist man. But it is also
attractive to those who believe in scientism. Julian Huxley, in his book
New Bottles for New Wine, published in 1950, wrote, "I believe in
transhumanism: once there are enough people who can truly say that,
the human species will be on the threshold of a new kind of existence,
as different from ours as ours is from that of Peking man. It will at
last be consciously fulfilling its real destiny."[6] Or to quote philosopher
Nick Bostrom, head of the Oxford Future of Humanity Institute:

> Transhumanism is a loosely defined movement that has
> developed gradually over the past two decades. It promotes
> an interdisciplinary approach to understanding and evalu-
> ating the opportunities for enhancing the human condition
> and the human organism opened up by the advancement
> of technology. Attention is given to both present technolo-
> gies, like genetic engineering and information technology,
> and anticipated future ones, such as molecular nanotech-
> nology and artificial intelligence.

The enhancement options being discussed include radical extension of human health-span, eradication of disease, elimination of unnecessary suffering, and augmentation of human intellectual, physical, and emotional capacities. Other transhumanist themes include space colonization and the possibility of creating superintelligent machines, along with other potential developments that could profoundly alter the human condition. The ambit is not limited to gadgets and medicine, but encompasses also economic, social, institutional designs, cultural development, and psychological skills and techniques.

Transhumanists view human nature as a work-in-progress, a half-baked beginning that we can learn to remold in desirable ways. Current humanity need not be the endpoint of evolution. Transhumanists hope that by responsible use of science, technology, and other rational means we shall eventually manage to become posthuman, beings with vastly greater capacities than present human beings have.[7]

This ideology of transhumanism often takes on one of two major themes: either that of *transhumanist utopianism* or that of *transhumanist anti-dystopianism.* The first theme of transhumanist utopianism is perhaps best exemplified by "futurist" Ray Kurzweil and his now popular notion of "the singularity." To quote Kurzweil, "Within a few decades, machine intelligence will surpass human intelligence, leading to The Singularity—technological change so rapid and profound it represents a rupture in the fabric of human history. The implications include the merger of biological and non-biological intelligence, immortal software-based humans, and the ultra-high levels of intelligence that expand outward in the universe at the speed of light."[8]

The second theme is that of transhumanist anti-dystopianism, which holds that we are facing imminent doom, but that transhumanism can save us. This view is perhaps best captured by philosopher Toby Ord, a senior research fellow at Oxford and author of a book on existential global crises, *The Precipice*. He says, "'The Precipice' is a time where we've reached the ability to pose existential risk to ourselves, which is substantially bigger than the natural risks, the background that we were facing before. And this is something where I now think that the risk is high enough, that this century, it's about one in six."[9]

So often the very same set of technocratic experts simultaneously purport to be cutting-edge technology innovators and also exemplars of technological prudence, care, and caution. According to these folks, the answer to our problems is a combination of technological innovation and massive regulation of everything and everyone by technologically minded bureaucrats.

Indeed, a 2019 *Business Insider* interview with Bostrom notes that "Under Bostrom's vision of mass surveillance, humans would be monitored *at all times* via artificial intelligence, which would send information to 'freedom centers' that work to save us from doom. To make this possible, he said, all humans would have to wear necklaces, or 'freedom tags,' with multi-directional cameras." According to Bostrom, "Obviously there are huge downsides and indeed massive risks to mass surveillance and global governance."[10] But apparently he thinks the risks are worth it because it will save us from catastrophe. It is the same sort of thinking that guided unparalleled government interference in our lives during the COVID-19 pandemic, that guides climate-change alarmists, and that university "experts" love to promote—all acting as our guardians. It brings to mind the words of the Roman poet Juvenal: *Quis custodiet ipsos custodes?* Who will guard the guards?

To those who believe in scientism, the answer to that question is always scientists, bureaucrats, and educated people like themselves operating from seats of power in world government. For instance, in his book *The Open Conspiracy: Blueprints for a World Revolution*, H. G. Wells envisions a world "politically, socially, and economically unified. Within that frame fall all the other ideas of our progressive ambition." That "ambition" is defined as "a world revolution aiming at universal peace, welfare, and happy activity" and "the establishment of a world directorate." This, in turn, requires recognizing the "provisional nature of all existing governments"; the replacement of "private, local, or national ownership of at least credit, transport, and staple production by a responsible world directorate"; the "practical recognition of the necessity for world biological controls, for example, of population and disease"; the "supreme duty of subordinating the personal career to the creation of a world directorate capable of these tasks and to the general advancement of human knowledge, capacity, and power." He adds: "the vision of a world at peace and liberated for an unending growth of knowledge and power is worth every danger of the way."[11]

In general, transhumanists believe that human beings are reducible to data points; technology can deliver secular utopia; tech gurus should lead society (and globalist technocrats manage it); and depopulation, anti-natalism, extreme life extension, vegetarianism/veganism, alternative sexual lifestyles, New Age spiritualism (but not Christianity), wokeism, and new-urbanist, "smart-city" living are all unquestionably good things. If this profile sounds familiar, it's because you might see a lot of it at universities, or in Big Tech, or filtering down into your neighbors, especially the ones with the signs in their front yards advertising that "In This House We Believe Science Is Real, Black Lives Matter, No Person Is Illegal, Love Is Love, Diversity Makes Us Stronger." In short, it is really a narcissistic cult, a cult first fostered in universities, that seeks to fill the superficial, atomized, and spiritually bereft condition of many modern Americans who lack an authentic sense of purpose, community, and identity—a condition certainly exacerbated by technology.

The real cure for this condition is Christianity and a classical liberal-arts education. But that's not what's on offer. What's on offer is an anti-Christian, anti-perennial philosophy and alleged techno-fix complete with the abolition of humanity (as Christians understand it) and the imposition of a rule-by-experts totalitarian government. Indeed, it is hard to see how transhumanist ideas of human "enhancement" aren't really about human "erasure." Even under Kurzweil's optimistic vision of creating a singularity between man's biology, robotics, and artificial intelligence, transhumanism sounds more like a case of *annihilation* of the human species as we know it and the creation of a new entity that will no longer be us. We might therefore wonder what would be the point of living endlessly as hybrid machines and why we should surrender our freedom to this end. Our limitedness, finitude, and imperfections are part of being human. What would be the point of creativity, courage, sacrifice, effort, responsibility, and all the things that make for human dignity if all our needs and comforts were perfectly met all the time? Transhumanism constitutes a diminishment of mankind, not an enhancement. But that's where the insanities of the university—all the incoherent wokeism and all the insidious scientism—are leading us. If that wasn't clear before, we hope it is now.

Islands in the Storm

So, are there still colleges where you can get a solid education without the insanity? Yes, there are handful, and others that deserve at least honorable mention for being better than the norm—which in itself takes an incredible effort of swimming against the tide.

Here's a non-exhaustive shortlist of colleges that we can, sometimes, with reservations, recommend, if you feel you must go to college. We've tried to include colleges and universities of different sizes, covering different academic interests, and in different regions of the country. Feel free to write to us with your own recommendations and comments:

Aquinas College, Tennessee
Auburn University, Alabama
Ave Maria University, Florida
Baylor University, Texas
Belmont Abbey College, North Carolina
Benedictine College, Kansas
Berry College, Georgia
Biola University, California
Brigham Young University, Utah
The Catholic University of America, Washington, D.C.
Cedarville University, Ohio
Christendom College, Virginia
The Citadel, South Carolina
Clemson University, South Carolina
College of the Ozarks, Missouri
Colorado Christian University, Colorado
Franciscan University of Steubenville, Ohio
Grove City College, Pennsylvania
Hampden-Sydney College, Virginia
Harding University, Arkansas
Hillsdale College, Michigan

Holy Apostles College, Connecticut
Houston Baptist University, Texas
John Paul the Great University, California
The King's College, New York
Liberty University, Virginia
Magdalen College of the Liberal Arts, New Hampshire
Oral Roberts University, Oklahoma
Patrick Henry College, Virginia
Pepperdine University, California
Regent University, Virginia
Saint Vincent College, Pennsylvania
Stonehill College, Massachusetts
Texas A&M University, Texas
Texas Christian University, Texas
Thomas Aquinas College, California
The Thomas More College of Liberal Arts, New Hampshire
United States Merchant Marine Academy, New York
United States Military Academy, New York
United State Naval Academy, Maryland
The University of Dallas, Texas
The University of Mary, North Dakota
The University of St. Thomas, Texas
The Virginia Military Institute, Virginia
Wofford College, South Carolina
Walsh University, Ohio
Wyoming Catholic College, Wyoming

None of these colleges are perfect. Some are more imperfect than others. All will have been touched in some way by the bad trends that afflict all higher education—or education, period, in the United States.

But we recognize that for some, higher education is a calling, something that should be undertaken, and for those select few (provided they guard their intellect and their character in these institutions as they would in any other), these schools represent possible alternatives because they retain, at least in part and as far as we can judge, some sense of academic integrity. Four years spent in these schools will not necessarily be four years wasted—especially if you attend with all our warnings in mind.

CHAPTER SEVEN

How to Teach Yourself Philosophy (and Do the Same for Other Subjects)

"No man who worships education has got the best out of education.... Without a gentle contempt for education no man's education is complete."

—G. K. Chesterton

So, suppose you've taken our advice. You've decided not to go to college. Let's go one step further and say that you've got a job or an apprenticeship and that part of your life, the economic part, is taken care of. But you still want to get a solid self-education in a hard academic discipline, like philosophy, the queen of the sciences.

You can do it—and you can do it quickly. And what you can do with a subject like philosophy, you can do for any other subject you want—English and American literature, history, religion, calculus, physics, or economics, you name it.

The basics of teaching yourself anything are relatively simple. It starts with defining your goal. The more narrowly you define it, the more you can go in-depth. The more broadly you define it, the more you'll aim for a broader overview, but never too broad. Your learning goal should be stateable in a single sentence. And that single sentence should have books that are specifically devoted to it. So, for instance, your learning goal can be as broad as a history of the world. In which case, you might turn to *The History of the World* by J. M. Roberts.

Or it might be as narrow as the works of T. S. Eliot, in which case you might start with a collection of his poems.

And because your time is valuable, set yourself a time limit: ninety days will work for most topics—again contingent on how you define them. Depending on your interests you could study a topic sequentially. For example, if you were interested in American history, you could do a broad overview or you could divide it into ninety-day study periods—on America's founding era, the Civil War, the twentieth century, and so on, however you wanted to divide it. One of the virtues of teaching yourself is that you set the agenda and the curriculum. Your interests and your goals are what will propel your intellectual journey. And your costs can be as low as buying a handful of cheap paperbacks (not those one-hundred-dollar academic-textbook monstrosities).

To get started, get a primer on the subject. You want something that's short and cuts through the chaff, quickly. The Intercollegiate Studies Institute (ISI Books) has published an excellent series of "A Student's Guide to" the following subjects: political philosophy, U.S. history, liberal learning, the study of history, economics, philosophy, literature, the core curriculum, American thought, classics, music history, the study of law, natural science, psychology, international relations, and religious studies. These books are all under a hundred pages and can help direct you to the sources you might want to tap. For something with a little more depth, you can start with Regnery Publishing's *Politically Incorrect Guide* series. These are meaty, provocative takes on big topics, including: American History, the Bible, the Sixties, Feminism, Western Civilization, the American Revolution, the Founding Fathers, the Constitution, the Civil War, American Presidents, Real American Heroes, Capitalism, Economics, Socialism, Global Warming, Climate Change, Science, Pandemics, Darwinism and Intelligent Design, the South, Hunting, the British Empire, English and American Literature, Immigration, Islam, Jihad, Communism, Christianity, and Catholicism. If you prefer a lecture format, there are also resources online, including our own online classes that offer both taped and live Zoom lectures on academic subjects ranging from philosophy to religion to history to law.

Once you stake out the parameters of a subject, it's easier to narrow your focus and get down to business. This is true even if the subject is enormous. Philosophy covers a vast expanse of history, intellectual schools, and ideas of the utmost complexity. Even if we narrow our focus to Western philosophy, we're looking at thinkers from Plato (fifth century BC) to, say, Roger Scruton in the late twentieth and early twenty-first century AD. And the material covered is not easy. In philosophy you'll be dealing with all sorts of fundamental issues of "what" and "why" and "how" that those less philosophically inclined simply ignore, relying instead on an unexamined philosophy that they've unthinkingly adopted as their own. It is true, as Cicero said, that "There is nothing so absurd but that some philosopher has not already said it."[1] But Cicero was a philosopher himself, a Stoic, so his point was not to condemn philosophy per se, but bad philosophers; and by teaching yourself you can steer clear of those while reading philosophers of lasting value. As philosopher and historian Will Durant pointed out, while we might live in a scientific age (in his case, in the twentieth century), philosophy remains the keystone subject of any intelligent person's life.

> Science always seems to advance, while philosophy seems always to lose ground. Yet this is only because philosophy accepts the hard and hazardous task of dealing with problems not yet open to methods of science—problems like good and evil, beauty and ugliness, order and freedom, life and death; so soon as a field of inquiry yields knowledge

susceptible to exact formulation it is called science. Every science begins as philosophy and ends as art; it arises in hypothesis and flows into achievement. Philosophy is a hypothetical interpretation of the unknown (as in metaphysics), or of the inexactly known (as in ethics or political philosophy); it is the front trench in the siege of truth. Science is the captured territory; and behind it are those secure regions in which knowledge and art build our imperfect and marvelous world.[2]

Science, as we've seen, is dependent on philosophy. Indeed, every aspect of our lives that involves thinking plunges us into philosophy, and every academic subject has a philosophical basis. But as is true with many subjects, the gist of philosophy can be boiled down to a simple question: What is truth? And if you want to answer that question without wasting your time or exploring answers that are uselessly abstruse, you can cut to the chase by reading the philosophers who set out the original questions and provided the answers that are still under debate. When you do that, you are looking at essentially two classical philosophers, Plato and Aristotle, and one from the Middle Ages, Saint Thomas Aquinas, who applied Aristotle to the world of Christian revelation.

There are of course many philosophers in between these and many who came after, but almost all of them wrote and spoke in response to Plato, Aristotle, or Aquinas. Ralph Waldo Emerson memorably said that "Out of Plato come all things that are still written and debated among men of thought.... Plato is philosophy, and philosophy, Plato."[3] "The safest general characterization of the European philosophical tradition is that it consists of a series of footnotes to Plato," according to Alfred North Whitehead.[4] He is where Western philosophy begins. Aristotle, meanwhile, is his great counterpoint.

As German philosopher Friedrich Schlegel said, "Every man is born either a Platonist or an Aristotelian."[5] And while that may be true, a man can go further and become a Thomist. Saint Thomas Aquinas Christianized Aristotle to shape the "perennial philosophy" that never goes out of date because it rests on eternal truths. So, if you want to get to the practical heart of philosophy, these are your go-to authors. A month with each would be time well spent. With Plato, you can narrow him down to one book: *The Republic*. Plato's philosophy—like Aristotle's and Aquinas's—is all-encompassing. But every author has his key text, and for Plato it is *The Republic*, which covers manifold aspects of Plato's thinking—everything from politics to ethics and metaphysics, from psychology to poetry and education (mental and physical)—as he applies it to envisioning the ideal republic.

Plato is a man of big ideas. So is Aristotle, but where Plato couches some of what he believes in narrative myths or abstract theorizing or Socratic dialogues, Aristotle is a man of the tangible, the down-to-earth, philosophical common sense, and "the golden mean." He believes in things we can learn by observation and experience and logic. While not a "scientist"—the scientific method was not yet established, and scientific methods of measurement were limited—he is in some ways one of the founders of modern science (which really didn't get under way until the Catholic Church took a hand in sponsoring science in its monasteries and newly invented universities).

Interestingly though, while of a "practical" bent, Aristotle is no more a "materialist" than Plato is. Both men believe that man's highest aspirations—and even his destiny—exist in a realm that we might call theological. They believe in objective truths—intellectual, moral, and scientific—and believe that these truths are part and parcel of and reveal a God-given world.

Aristotle is harder to condense into a single volume than is Plato, but two texts might suffice, Aristotle's *Politics* and his *Ethics*. Aristotle was Plato's student, and while Plato imagined the ideal republic, Aristotle tutored Alexander the Great, ruler of what was—to the Greeks—the known world. Without going to college, you can give yourself the same tutor that Alexander the Great had!

If Plato will provide you with the best sort of midnight student–bull sessions about the meaning of life (at a level you won't ever get at a real college campus and with genuine worth that has stood the test of time over more than two millennia), Aristotle will give you a crash course in logic, in making sure that what you say adds up and can withstand the severest scrutiny of real-world applications. If Plato is in some sense an idealist (though you may not find all his ideals admirable), Aristotle is a realist (though you may not find all of his realism acceptable). Plato and Aristotle are challenging authors not in the sense of being inherently difficult—they walk you through their philosophy step by step—but because their ideas will likely challenge many of your own lazy preconceptions. That was one reason why they once formed the backbone of a liberal arts education.

Then comes the giant Aquinas, a man of encyclopedic knowledge and sanctity whose *Summa Theologica* is a perennial catechism. It is far too long to tackle in a month, but there are abbreviated versions that you can set as your main text. *Aquinas's Shorter Summa* is a good, modern rendition of Aquinas's own condensation of his work; *Thomas Aquinas: Selected Writings* is another good choice; and *The Aquinas Catechism* and Peter Kreeft's *Summa of the Summa* are also excellent.[6] And there are others. Go to a bookstore, browse, and choose the translation that works for you. Once you've finished with your month-long study, you can consider doing a deeper dive.

In Aquinas, you will get the best of Aristotle positioned within a Christian context; you will be confronted with the biggest questions any man has to answer; and you will find yourself immersed in the saint's own compelling way of argument that subjects statements to objections and objections to rebuttals in a disciplined question-and-answer format dedicated to finding objective truth. In Aquinas you will learn a logical case for the existence of God, what we can know of God's nature, and much else besides. As we say, his knowledge is encyclopedic. And like an encyclopedia his knowledge is presented in such a fashion that it is meant to be applied. He is a model of fairness, of clearly stated and soundly articulated arguments and counterarguments. He is an apostle of truth. Get a grasp on Aquinas and you are well-set with a philosophy of life.

Does that exhaust any need to study philosophy further? No, of course not, but remember that most college students will never read any Plato or Aristotle or (especially) Aquinas at all. The fact is that for everyone, whether college graduate or autodidact, learning is a *lifelong* experience that you need to command yourself. You will go farther in any topic—and learn much more—the sooner you learn that. If you don't go to college, or if you teach yourself, you'll learn that much faster and with much less waste of time on books and lectures of dubious (or negative) value.

Are there other philosophers worth studying? Certainly, but that depends on your learning goals. Some of us, like the authors of this book, have had to study certain philosophers if only to understand how wrong those philosophers were—often ludicrously, catastrophically wrong. But you might not have the time for that, or the interest. In which case, stick to what is essential and true.

But let's make things more challenging. Suppose you want a *post-graduate* level of knowledge in a subject. You might suppose that would be impossible. But, no, it is very possible, for the same reason (that learning is a lifelong experience) and using the very same tools of defining your goals and assigning yourself the proper texts.

Let's take a hard case. Let's assume you wanted to focus on where philosophy went wrong, where it started taking on the neo-Marxism that has corrupted our universities and is systematically destroying them and turning them into indoctrination centers dedicated to laying waste to American and Western civilization. If, as we say, sanity lies with the Thomistic understanding of philosophy, how do we get back there? How do we undo the philosophic errors that brought us to our current state?

Talk about a big topic. But it's not that hard to tackle. Once you've undertaken an overview of philosophy, you'll know when, historically, the anti-Thomists began their major offensive. The answer is in the seventeenth and eighteenth centuries. That's when under the combined pressures of the Reformation (which overthrew Europe's Christian unity) and the Enlightenment (which separated reason from revelation), you not only had the cataclysm of the French Revolution, but you had a long (and ongoing) assault on Thomism and the whole idea of objective Christian truth and the very roots of Western civilization.

Undertaking the study of this big topic is a great thing, because once you see how truth was subverted, you can go back and undo it—perhaps in your own mind, and even in society. What once was can always be again. It's only leftists, with their fetish of "progress," who deny that obvious truth, always cast the past in a negative light, and tell us we "can't turn back the clock" or that we're "on the wrong side" of ever-progressive history. They don't want you to know the truth about the past, about philosophy, about much of anything. They have their own catechism, and it is one of determinist-materialist atheism coupled with an incoherent ethic of unrelenting egalitarianism. We believe that every human being should be educated according to the rational, moral nature of man. They believe that man is a demigod of self-creation with no nature, and that science and technology, bureaucrats and experts, can refashion him in a way that will fulfill every human need, meet every human desire, and achieve secular utopia.

If you've undertaken your own basic study of philosophy, you will already have absorbed what is stated in the New World Encyclopedia about the relationship between Aristotelianism and Thomism:

> Thomism is the philosophical school that followed in the legacy of Thomas Aquinas. The word comes from the name of its originator, whose summary work *Summa Theologiae* has arguably been second only to the Bible in importance to the Catholic Church. During the thirteenth century, the [Aristotelian] philosophy of ancient Greece was introduced to European scholars through the works of Arabian and Jewish scholars, and the works of Aristotle became available for the first time in Latin translation. Thomas Aquinas synthesized the principles of Aristotle with the doctrines of the Christian faith, using logic and dialectic to produce an explanation of Catholic dogma. The thought of Thomas Aquinas was important in shifting medieval philosophy (also known as Scholasticism) away from the influence of Plato and towards Aristotle. The ensuing school of thought became one of the most influential philosophies of all time, through its influence on Roman Catholicism and Catholic ethics, and through the sheer number of people who lived by its teachings.
>
> In the Encyclical *Doctoris Angelici* (1914), Pope Pius X cautioned that the teachings of the Catholic Church cannot be understood without the basic philosophical underpinning of Aquinas's major theses. The Second Vatican Council described Aquinas'[s] system as the "Perennial Philosophy."[7]

This summary reveals that not only is it possible to "turn back the clock," but the perennial philosophy has not been extinguished—it lives on in the largest religion with the most universal scope in the world, the Catholic Church. That's something to build on.

From your previous study of philosophy, you will know that the rise of the great Athenian philosopher Plato centered on his solution to the problem of change, which stymied pre-Athenian Greek philosophy. The pre-Socratic philosophers believed that the universe was composed of a single element but disagreed as to what that element was.[8] The most important of these pre-Socratic philosophers were Parmenides and Heraclitus, who sought to explain why living and inanimate objects both appeared to change in this single element universe.

Parmenides believed that change was an illusion,[9] and that the fundamental force of the universe was *being* or *stasis*.[10] Heraclitus believed that the fundamental force of the universe was *becoming* or *flux*.[11] In short, "Parmenides took the view that nothing changes in reality; only our senses [deceptively] convey the appearance of change. Heraclitus, by contrast, thought that everything changes all the time, and that we 'step and do not step into the same river,' for new waters flow ever about us."[12] According to Heraclitus "there is nothing of which we may say, 'it is,'" and the belief that anything is "persistent" is "error and foolishness."[13] For Heraclitus, everything perishes and nothing remains.

So Greek philosophy was divided "between those who seek permanence (the stasis of Parmenides) and those who embrace change (the flux of Heraclitus)."[14] It was Plato who broke this false dichotomy by showing how change and stasis could coexist. Plato conceived of *two* coexistent realms: one corresponding closely with Parmenidean stasis and the other with Heraclitean flux. Plato vindicated both of these thinkers, while placing them in a greater context. They saw partial truths of which Plato asserted a whole.

Plato posited that there was a realm of permanence, stasis, and unity. It belonged to what he categorized as the realm of *form*. There was also, he averred, a realm of flux, change, and decay that pertains to the realm of *matter*. Form and matter, as you've learned from your study of philosophy, are basic philosophical categories, introduced by Plato and refined by Aristotle. They can be summarized here:

> The terms **form** and **matter** describe a basic duality in all existence, between the essence or "whatness" of a thing (form) and the stuff that the thing is made of (matter). That such a duality exists is widely held, but the definitions of form and matter have differed throughout the history of philosophy; hence a precise definition of each will differ depending on the specific philosophical system.
>
> In general, though, the terms form and matter derive from classical philosophy, most significantly from Plato and Aristotle. In Plato form comes from the Greek word *eidos* and is often translated as idea or essence and refers to the basic "whatness" of a thing. Aristotle likewise links form to essence but distinguishes between form and matter where form refers to the essential determination or organic structure of a thing while matter is that which the thing is made of. The Scholastics incorporated the use of form and matter while making certain developments.
>
> Modern philosophy has largely rejected the classical Aristotelian concept.[15]

That rejection, as you'll see as your studies continue, is part of the problem.

Plato, however, had his own problem. He struggled to articulate how form and matter interact because he regarded form as divorced from matter. It was, as you know, Plato's student Aristotle who solved the problem.

Raphael's famous fresco *The School of Athens* places pre-Athenian philosophers—including Parmenides and Heraclitus—on the periphery of the foreground while Plato and Aristotle dominate the center. Plato and Aristotle engage each other eye-to-eye, but Plato points upward, while Aristotle points downward. Plato points to what is sometimes called the "noetic heaven," the realm of the forms, which are removed from the world of matter (though they make the material world intelligible).

Aristotle points to the earth, to matter, positing a view called "hylomorphism," meaning that form is "in" the matter of things. As you might remember, Aristotelianism invokes four causes—material, formal, efficient, and final—to explain what we find in the world. The material and formal causes more or less align with Plato's categories of matter and form. Form gives us our definition of, our ability to recognize, what a chair *is*. Matter explains its organic substance (wood). The efficient cause explains *how* the chair came together, the actions of its builder. The final cause explains *why* the chair was built, the *purpose* or *goal* for which it was built, to sit upon.

Another Aristotelian innovation was his answer to Parmenides's skepticism about the existence of change. Aristotle argued that the opposite of *being* (or actuality) is *potency* (or potential). Change is the process of potential being actualized.[16] In this formulation, Aristotle calculated the necessity of God, the unmoved mover, who initiates the actualization of potential and who exists outside of space and time.

In your sixty-day survey of Plato and Aristotle you might have come to this (proper) conclusion: Aristotle *ended* Greek philosophy. Nearly no one teaches philosophy this way, but it is, as you could have deduced from reading your assigned texts, a simple fact. Aristotle ended Greek philosophy because he answered the question that began it: "Does change exist in the universe, and, if so, how does it operate?" Aristotle answered that question and brought Greek philosophical inquiry to a satisfying and definitive close.

But Aristotle did something else besides. He provided Thomas Aquinas with the first of his five logical arguments for proving God's existence, the so-called "argument from change (or motion)."[17] After Aristotle philosophy naturally and logically gave way to theology, which was why, in your self-taught undergraduate course of philosophy, your readings took you from Plato to Aristotle to Aquinas.

Aquinas "baptized" Aristotelianism by showing how it applied to elements of the Christian life such as the Eucharist, the human soul, ethics, virtue, and a logically demonstrable existence of a single God. From the end of the thirteenth century up until the Reformation and the Enlightenment, Aristo-Thomism constituted what amounted to a "great education." If you spent your ninety days of studying philosophy as we recommended, you've got that, or the beginnings of it.

Now comes the graduate course in where philosophy went wrong. It starts with the "mechanical philosophy" of the Enlightenment. It sought, to lift a phrase from the Anglican empirical philosopher and statesman Francis Bacon, a "great instauration"[18]—a grand intellectual reconfiguration built upon a wholly new foundation. The first step was "dehellenizing" Western philosophy (which meant dismissing Plato and Aristotle, and in the process Thomism), and reformulating it around something else.[19] At first, this something else was "science," but science eventually gave way in the course of the nineteenth to twenty-first centuries to political ideologies, including today's "intersectional" neo-Marxism.

Francis Bacon, the father of modern scientism, believed that "knowledge of nature derives from observation and perception by the senses," meaning philosophers could restore man's intellect to its status prior to the Fall of Adam and Eve.[20] You read that right. For Francis Bacon, philosophy had gone wrong beginning with the fall of man. Everything that followed that was not based *empiricism*, on sensory knowledge, was wrong.

Reformation and Enlightenment philosophers made common cause to reject the past and the Aristo-Thomism of the Catholic Church. The Protestants rejected Aristotle as a pagan. The Enlightenment *philosophes* because he was old and insufficiently "scientific." Protestants rejected Saint Thomas Aquinas because he was Catholic—and so did the Enlightenment *philosophes*. Both characterized the dynamic Middle Ages, in which a Christian civilization was built out of the ruins of Rome, as the "Dark Ages"—a way to flatter themselves. Bacon wrote two great treatises, *Instauratio Magna* and the more famous *Novum Organum*, which was self-consciously intended to displace Aristotle's work on logic entitled *Organon*.

Even philosophers who want to start anew build on previous works, and Bacon was influenced by what philosophers call *nominalism*, a late medieval critique of Plato (and by implication Aristotle and Thomism) that was skeptical about the real existence, outside the human mind, of the Platonic forms. Aristotle's (and Aquinas's) solution to this problem that form and matter were one was regarded as suspect or insufficient. In truth, Aristotle's unpopularity among Reformation and Enlightenment philosophers had nothing to do with his ideas being insufficiently tested (Aristotle ranks among the world's great philosophical rigorists), rather his ideas stood athwart currents in Reformation and Enlightenment thought. The Reformation imposed both a form of subjectivism (every man his own priest) and intellectual limitation (*sola scriptura*, by scripture alone) that made Aristotle's pagan objective philosophy unwelcome. Similarly, Aristotle was a down-to-earth realist about man and politics, and that made him an intellectual opponent of the Enlightenment's superstitious belief in refashioning man and seeking after utopia.

As is well known, but far less often taught, Bacon's philosophy was influenced by "occultism," alchemy (the idea that mercury could be mixed with other metals to modify their chemical composition and create gold),[21] corpuscularianism ("the mechanical philosophy" in which magical particles called corpuscles act like bewitched atoms effecting changes, including chemical, physical changes such as those sought by alchemists),[22] and an esoteric interpretation of nature. Bacon's methods, indeed, may be seen as "correspond[ing] to those of astrology in an attempt to discover the relationship of man to the stars and how to exploit that knowledge to obtain health, wealth, and immortality."[23] In the search for a new foundation for knowledge, magical potions and incantations, mystical crystals, and outright witchcraft reside uncomfortably close to Bacon's founding of "modern science" and to the thinking of other Enlightenment philosophers like Robert Boyle, Pierre Gassendi, René Descartes, and Isaac Newton.

While dabbling with an occult view of nature, the Enlightenment philosophers promoted themselves as empiricists and rationalists, and to that end they rejected two of Aristotle's causes—the formal (what defines a chair as a chair) and the final (what defines its purpose, for sitting). They held that the only empirical, rational causes are matter (the material a chair is made of) and the efficient (how it is built). The formal and final causes were thought to be too metaphysical. That should be a hint of the dangerous, foolish reductionism of modern philosophy, because to any commonsensical view, Aristotle's formal and final causes are self-evident and plainly sensible. This "determinist," "rationalist," "materialist," distrust or outright rejection of "metaphysics"—whether Aristotelian or Thomistic—is the beginning of the road to popular atheism and our modern philosophical and social insanity.

Francis Bacon and René Descartes believed that by excluding formal and final causation their new study of physics would be purely "scientific," relying solely on material and efficient causes. Descartes "rejected substantial forms and final causes in physics"[24] because he wanted to exclude anything he could neither measure nor see. He thus rejected "teleological explanations"—explanations of design or purpose—"in natural philosophy."[25] Cartesian rationalism (the idea that all knowledge comes from reason rather than from experience, tradition, or revelation) and Baconian empiricism (the idea that knowledge is reducible to what we can experience with our senses) more or less created Enlightenment scientism.[26]

From your study of Plato and Aristotle, you can see that we've just gone back to square one. If you eliminate the realm of forms, if you eliminate Aristotle's final cause, then we're thrown back, in some ways to the pre-Socratic philosopher Heraclitus and the idea of everything being in constant flux. That's a great philosophy if you want to justify relativism, reject eternal truth, and ultimately deny God. There are other implications too.

By removing Aristotle's understanding that form and matter are one, you remove the idea that man is a composite of body and soul. Both are necessary to make a man. Aristotle believed that and so do Christians. It explains why Christian theology insists on a bodily resurrection. Those who reject Aristotle and Saint Thomas Aquinas, however, have an extremely difficult time explaining soul and body, mind and brain, consciousness and action; it explains why followers of modern scientism (and some Reformation Protestants) deny free will; it even explains why the LGBTQ+ movement and the transhumanist movement believe that bodies and "identities" can and should be whatever we want them be: to them the body (biological reality) is a prison from which subjective choice and technological interventions can free us. If you ever wondered how apparently "academic" or "abstract" philosophy can have real-world implications—vast real-world implications—you've just seen it.

Of course, the implications reveal themselves over time. In the classic formulation of Richard Weaver, "Ideas have consequences." Karl Marx and Charles Darwin, for instance, advanced the idea that man and the world are fundamentally, even exclusively, *material*. Darwin's theory of evolution, for example, with its account of man arising from the incremental aggregation of random biological mutations and blind, deterministic accidents, functioned to unseat man as a created being situated within a divinely organized and purposeful universe,[27] while making him different only *in degree* from the higher-ordered beasts all the way down to the primordial ooze. As a matter of "science" divorced from Christian conceptions of morality, Darwin's theory of evolution laid the groundwork for eugenics and "Social Darwinist" programs to make use of this science in ways that would advance human "progress," (along with eliminating those judged "unfit"). It was once thought that eugenics was discredited because of the National Socialists (the Nazis), who made it a centerpiece of their progressive program. But as we've seen, eugenics has simply rebranded itself, again, as scientific progress, which can eliminate certain classes of people (like those with Down's Syndrome) and provide designer babies for the wealthy or the infertile or those who practice homosexuality.

Karl Marx, for his part, was even more the materialist—explicitly atheistic and reducing man to little more than a unit of labor and production, alienated from his work, exploited, and duty-bound to rise up and revolt against the exploiter capitalist class. His ideology of envy and violence, of class hatred and class enemies, of revolution and the dictatorship, has proven to be the deadliest and most evil in the history of mankind, with a death toll of near one hundred million. But despite that historical record, Marxism, updated with the addition of intersectionality, is the ideology that dominates college campuses. This was the work of a dedicated cadre of neo-Marxists from the so-called "Frankfurt School," one of the most famous of whom was Antonio Gramsci, who wrote: "Socialism is precisely the religion that must overwhelm Christianity.... In the new order, Socialism will triumph by first capturing the culture via infiltration of schools, universities, churches, and the media by transforming the consciousness of society."[28]

Where philosophy went wrong was in turning against Saint Thomas Aquinas and Aristotle, and ultimately turning against Christianity. You could get that from an intelligent, critical reading of a history of philosophy; and your ability to analyze that history could come straight from your ninety-day course in the perennial philosophy because you would know how to analyze arguments and find truth.

Are there other philosophical avenues to explore? Yes, many, including Friedrich Nietzsche, one of the most influential philosophers of the nineteenth and twentieth centuries, a man full of profound insights but also of literal insanity. His infamous proclamation that "God is dead" and his ideas about "the will to power," "master versus slave mentality," and the "Übermensch" are often linked to National Socialism.

Just as Aristotle and Saint Thomas Aquinas gave us the perennial philosophy, so too is philosophy a perennial subject. There is always more to read and more to learn, including more falsehoods to rebut. The perennial philosophy is your plumb line, your true north, as you navigate ideas in whatever courses you set yourself. And that process of learning is a lifelong process.

What is true for studying philosophy or literature can be applied to everything from learning a language to learning carpentry. "Do it yourself" is not just a slogan, it can be a way of life. For the self-taught man, it is the most rewarding way of life. And with this book, you now have some of the tools you need to get the job done.

CHAPTER EIGHT

Double-Agentry: How to Subvert the Radicals (If You Must Go to College)

"One man who would stop lying could bring down a tyranny."

—Aleksandr Solzhenitsyn

If by some misfortune you have no choice but to go to college, because you need to go to an advanced trade school—like law school or medical school or business school—or because your engineering or science interests dictate it, or because you thought it worth trying one of our (somewhat) recommended schools, we understand. But we also warn you. You will need to be a double agent. With rare exceptions, you will likely be in a covert (or maybe even overt) political, philosophical war with your university professors and administrators. You need to accept this fact. There should be no misunderstandings. You cannot just go along and get along. You will need to give the radicals a taste of their own medicine. They gained power not through right reason, but by throwing tantrums. Granted, the tantrums they threw had the sympathy of clueless campus liberals who thought their tantrums were about tolerance and free speech and oppressed minorities. You won't have that advantage. You are the minority they want to oppress, to whom they would deny free speech, for whom they have no tolerance. But you can still outmaneuver them. Remember: You are *not* in *a dialogue* with these folks. In fact, you never were. Leftists mouth support for "tolerance" only when they don't have power enough to impose their will. Every leftist appeal to mutual, reciprocal respect, open-mindedness, truth-seeking, common ground, and pluralism is just a tactic to keep you in check while they take social, political, and institutional power and turn it against you.

If you are a student intent on staying in college, you must realize that you cannot defend your beliefs to these people on the basis of logic, evidence, and sound argumentation. You still need all these things, but that's for you, for your own understanding. Just don't expect the radicals to regard you as anything other than a class threat against whom unjust discrimination is not only valid but necessary.

If you really want to make a difference, you must be willing *to take over* your classroom and campus. You must be willing *to start being feared.* And you must be willing to turn your campus into an arms race of litigious and semi-litigious slip-and-fall theatrics, just like the Left did and continues to do so successfully. The Left is not used to having opposition on campus. They will overreact—they always do—and you should be ready to record and broadcast their overreactions. Exposing them for the gender-obsessed lunatics they really are is the best way to get a countervailing wind blowing on college campuses. When parents and conservative alumni and state legislators are forced to get a whiff of what is really going on—something they studiously try to avoid for their own peace of mind—even they can feel pressured to protest, and good things can happen.

Before attempting any of these stunts, it is important to go over the ground rules. First, we're *not* going to play entirely as the Left does. Unlike their thugs, we promote only *nonviolent* forms of protest. We believe in *civil* disobedience and *humorous* social mischief. Dress well. Groom yourself well. Be articulate. Show courage. Don't ever back down. Be a man of principle. And spend your time wisely. If you can find conservative professors, attend their classes. Stuff your class schedule with the most demanding, intellectually challenging, old-school academic courses you can, if you have teachers who are actually there to teach and not proselytize for the insane Left.

Be a man of action: politely but firmly call on congressmen, state legislators, and local officials to immediately cut taxpayer funding to all the evil, woke intersectionality programs on college campuses. Although our tactics go far beyond the comfortable and the easy, get your "sea legs" by writing for the conservative student newspaper. Although this is not anywhere *near* enough to turn the tide, this is how conservative media stars Dinesh D'Souza and Laura Ingraham, entrepreneur Peter Thiel, U.S. senator Ted Cruz, and scholars Yoram Hazony and Charles Kessler got their starts. Become a public speaker, constantly informing church groups, civic groups, and any group that will have you about how truly corrupt and insane the present university system has become. To deserve our tax dollars—let alone your tuition—universities must do a lot better.

To do what we call for as a student activist, you'll need a thick skin. You'll need to have a mischievous attitude. And you'll need friends. Think of Samuel Adams and the Sons of Liberty. *Don't go it alone.* For one thing, there is safety in numbers. Second, performing these actions will be more fun and effective if done with others. It will also be an energizing reminder to onlookers that we are not alone, and that some of us are no longer willing to be the silent minority. Show some backbone and you might find some secret allies. For conservative students interested in these right-wing social guerrilla tactics, you just need to remember this twofold goal:

1. *Make your leftist professors, deans, fellow students, and administrators scared of you*
2. *Waste as much of their time and victim-mongering resources as possible*

That's it. Those are your objectives.

With those two overarching ends in mind, here's what you need to do.

Seven Principles for Reclaiming (or Collapsing) Your College or University

1. The Classroom Is Your Stage, the Campus Is Your Theatre

Anyone who stays in college must remember Walt Whitman's immortal words, "the powerful play goes on, and you may contribute a verse."[1] The campus is your theater, the classroom is your stage, and you need to master the techniques of what we call *Counter-Revolutionary Classroom Guerilla Melodrama* (or CRCGM for short). It will make demure fellow travelers in the classroom admire you, hapless passersby marvel at you, and brainwashed leftist classmates hate you (that's all right, you need enemies to sharpen you). Most important, it will make your professors and administrators fear you.

Play to their effete liberalism. Point out that you are, in fact, the *victim—always* and *everywhere*. If you are a straight, white, Christian male, you get zero minority privilege on the intersectionality chart. So, take advantage of that and point out that you are the one, the only, the truly oppressed class on campus. Your opponents are guilty of *ancestorism*, blaming you for the all the great things your ancestors allegedly did—like building the greatest civilization and the greatest, most prosperous, and freest country on earth (and also the most generous, as you're even willing to share it with others who are legal citizens and want to read the Great Books and support traditional Christian ideals).

Remember that *acting is reacting*, and every time your professor ignores your "minority" status—or says something typically inane in class—you and your friends should take theatrical umbrage. This is the heart of CRCGM.

2. Control Classroom Demographical Language

No matter the academic discipline that is being "taught" in most college classrooms today, race and ethnicity will by design be mixed in with the course's content. Even if it only presents itself as a first-day question along the lines of, "By show of hand, how many of you identify as persons of color?"

This is your time to shine. Know your cues. If your professor refers to you as "white," angrily demand that he call you "European American," shouting your ethnic pride angrily from your seat. If he calls you "Caucasian," take voluble umbrage and demand to be called "white." If he calls you "African American," insist that he refer to you as "black." If he calls you a "person of color," tell him you regard "color" as a racist term, reminding you of how segregationists separated out colored people, and that your preferred ethnic reference is "American" since you are a citizen and your people have been here for generations.

If race doesn't come up, "gender" will. Never use the word "transgender." Always insist that the correct word is "transvestite." When the professor asks for your pronouns, identify yourself by your hair color as someone who must be referred to as Golden-haired Thor, or Brown-haired Gladiator-for-Truth, or Ginger-haired Celtic-Avenger, or Black-haired Apache-Appropriator, and let your professor know that stating one's hair color is as important as stating your gender identity, in order to help the visually impaired, according to Microsoft.[2] And whenever he ignores your pronoun, insist on it. It's no more (or less) ridiculous than Zie, Zir, or the current flavor of the month, and LQBTQ+ sets no pronoun-definition boundaries. Everyone who hasn't had commonsense "educated" out of them, knows that the whole pronoun performance routine is an idiotic, degrading exercise in how much compliance a leftist can enforce on a liberal. So expose it.

3. Dramatize, Dramatize, Dramatize

Your professors will furnish you many "scene-setting" opportunities. Take advantage of them. Be ready with your skits. One could play out something like this:

> Professor: "Could I see the hands of all those who identify as persons of color?"
>
> You: "What do you mean by 'persons of color'?"
>
> Professor: "I meant non-whites, Kip. You're white, so it's good you didn't raise your hand."
>
> You: "What did you just call me? Did you say 'white'? Do you know how offensive that is? Do you know what it means?"
>
> Friend #1: "I'm sorry, professor, I'm not trying to make trouble. But as a neutral party here, I heard what you called him. We all did. You called him white. You outright said it. You called him a name—and if the administration asks me, I'll have to tell them. I might even have to volunteer the information."
>
> You: "All my life I've had to live with this—people calling me 'pigment-deprived.' My Uncle Rico nearly killed himself when someone called him what you just called me—as if

his life didn't matter, as if my life didn't matter. If you think I'm not reporting this, you're crazy, you're a crazy racist!"
Friend #2: "Look, I know his uncle really did consider suicide. There's a family history of post-traumatic stress disorder here, dating back to the riots. Kip deals with serious anxiety issues about his color. You need to apologize, to mitigate the damage. We all heard what you said. We all saw the hateful intent. Now, just sit down, Kip. I know she'll apologize; she'll make this right."
Professor: "I'm not apologizing."
You: "Rico! Rico! Say his name! I won't deny my ethnic heritage on account of your hatred—I'm proud of white people. How about I list all our cultural achievements? You're so blinded by racism you can't even see what my people have done. Do you know the extent to which Catholics have been discriminated against in this country? I'm reporting you to the administration—and I'm doing it right now—and then I'm going to report you to Tucker Carlson! And then I'm going to tell the newspaper that this crumby school discriminates against Roman Catholic Italian Americans. Why not ask me if my relatives are Sicilian, or in the mafia? Or by white do you mean to deny me my ethnic heritage? I'm outta here, man."

After you leave Friend #2 says: "Look, professor: we all understand that your racial slur just slipped out. But you had the chance to take it all back, and you squandered it. This is gonna end really badly for you."

The professor will respond with something worthless, but if you play your roles well enough, she will be feeling embarrassed and a bit sheepish by now. Guaranteed. The trick is this: there is no compendium of official "racist" terms—masterminds of the cultural Left reconfigure them annually. Whatever your professor (whom you want to get fired) calls you is the new racist term you've weaponized against her. This tactic simply cannot fail.

4. Get Two Radical Professors Fired: "Believe All Students"

Naturally, the mechanism of all the fear you've created in items 1–3 is termination. Work to get *no fewer than two* of your most anti-Christian, anti-morality, anti-white, anti-American professors fired. To do this, you must follow through on your in-class performances. Do so by petitioning the dean, the university's middle management, the HR department, and even local news with your stories of oppression, bigotry, and actual hatred at the hands of your professor-oppressors. The professors will usually happily cooperate, by the way. Just record some of their lectures and air them out in the world. Don't be intimidated by your radical professors or let them silence you. Rally behind the motto "Believe all students!" It will tip your opponents off-balance. Professors aren't used to being challenged. They will overreact. Keep your cool. They won't keep theirs.

And look, if this point sounds onerous, we get it. But remember the title of this book is *Don't Go to College*! If you choose to go that route, then go all the way and fight the fight, and do your part to get the bad guys fired. Your two most radical professors are willful defilers of parental trust, intentional corrupters of youth, and express enemies of the Christian West. Neither of your authors expected any mercy when we occupied the enemy's territory, and we received none. Today, radical professors expect no repercussions for their outrages. We need to change that.

5. They Take Down One of Ours, We Take Down Two of Theirs

A pastime of radical professors is to use their lectures to "take down" venerated historical figures—at least *our* historical figures. Theirs get a pass. No longer.

The definition of "our" historical figures is very broad. But then American patriotism used to be very broad, incorporating everyone from Christopher Columbus and Junípero Serra to Benjamin Franklin, George Washington, Thomas Jefferson, John Adams, Andrew Jackson, Ulysses Grant, and Robert E. Lee. That's the point. Patriotism is unifying.

But the Left is only interested in playing the intersectionality game to divide and, they think, conquer. But some of their tactics can be turned against them. So, when a leftist professor tries to disparage the polymath and founding-father achievements of, say, Benjamin Franklin (because he might have had amorous affairs) or Thomas Jefferson (because some allege that he kept a slave mistress), bring up someone your professor will have to defend.

For instance, how about Martin Luther King Jr.? He has a national holiday that, like Jackie Robinson Day in baseball, has become less about celebrating the ideal of a color-blind America (which we're now told is not "anti-racist" enough) and much more about promoting ever-lasting racial grievances.

But guess what? Martin Luther King Jr. seems to have had his own extramarital affairs, a lot of them, and some of them were apparently quite nasty. Unlike Franklin, the evidence against whom is merely circumstantial, or Jefferson, where it is still disputed, we now know that King was caught with "dozens of women" by American law enforcement on recorded audio tape![3] According to author David Garrow, who won a 1987 Pulitzer Prize for his biography of King: "newly revealed FBI documents portray the great civil rights leader as a sexual libertine who 'laughed' as a forcible rape took place."[4]

Garrow notes that "the full extent of the FBI's surveillance of the civil rights leader Dr. Martin Luther King.... [exposes] in graphic detail the FBI's intense focus on King's extensive extramarital sexual relationships with dozens of women, and also his presence in a Washington hotel room when a friend, a Baptist minister, allegedly raped one of his 'parishioners,' while King 'looked on, laughed, and offered advice.' The FBI's tape recording of that criminal assault still exists today, resting under court seal in a National Archives vault." Garrow continues: "The complete transcripts and surviving recordings are not due to be released until 2027, but when they are made fully available a painful historical reckoning concerning King's personal conduct seems inevitable."[5]

Let your professor—and classroom—know that if he thinks Franklin or Jefferson are to be disparaged for their tenuous, alleged infidelities, what King did was much worse.

This is the way. Take down their heroes as they take down ours. Educate yourself about the many, many sins of leftist heroes. Paul Johnson's book *Intellectuals* is one place to start.

6. You Are Not in a Dialogue

We reiterate this point, because it is so important and because the natural tendency of conservative students is to try to reason with their political opponents. Maybe in another public setting, or in your home, or amongst your friends you can do that. But in your left-wing classroom, on your left-wing campus, under left-wing academia's thought-policing...don't kid yourself. They won't engage with you rationally, they will only attack your motives as racist, sexist, homophobic, or whatever. Or they'll deploy "the motte-and-bailey fallacy" to channel you into a quagmire where reasoned argument is nearly impossible.[6] The motte-and-bailey fallacy, first coined by philosopher

Nicholas Shackel, is where your opponent makes two claims: a "motte" claim that is easily defended and a "bailey" claim that is not, but that can hide behind the motte claim. If the motte claim is not refuted, then the arguer can proceed as if the bailey claim is not refuted either. Consider, for instance, the following example.

Motte claim: "I believe in progress and we need to recognize past racism."

Bailey claim: "We need mandatory critical race theory training in every school."

The way to defeat the motte-and-bailey fallacy is to recognize the motte claim when it is deployed and flip the script. So when your opponent asks, "Don't you believe in progress?" you should say:

"No. I believe in natural law."

"Don't you think slavery was wrong?"

"Yes, of course, because it was a violation of natural law, in a grave but less egregious way than, say, abortion is."

"Don't you think you have privilege because of slavery?"

"No. *Every* citizen of the United States is somewhat privileged. But presently, American blacks and other 'persons of color' are the most privileged under affirmative action. Look it up."[7]

A motte-and-bailey argument is a battle over who can set the terms of debate. Don't let your opponents set the terms. And don't try to convince them either. Just throw dirt into the gears of their argument—and tell them they need to research more and to be more open-minded, tolerant, and rational.

7. State the Truth

The truth is on our side. So stop being complicit in the Left's lies. As Aleksandr Solzhenitsyn wrote: "*Never knowingly support lies! . . . Let us not glue back the flaking scales of the Ideology, not gather back its crumbling bones, nor patch together its decomposing garb, and we* will be amazed how swiftly and helplessly the lies will fall away, and that which is destined to be naked will be exposed as such to the world."[8]

Speak truth on your campus and in your classrooms and watch the ivory tower of lies begin to sway.

For the past seventy years, conservative students have gone to college to get an education, graduate, and go into the working world, while leftist progressives went to college to stay and take it over. They have fully accomplished that mission. They have done so not by way of truth, or logic, or reason, or evidence, or better arguments, but by employing a strategy of playing perpetual victim and by using an entire arsenal of violent, subversive, duplicitous, and social-engineering tactics to advance their neo-Marxist ends. The result, sadly, is that America's university system has become an archipelago of clown colleges.

Your best strategy is to sidestep them, don't give them your cash, and don't waste your time in them. But if you must go, you must be prepared to fight, and fight in ways that might cut against your natural inclinations. If you're going to make a difference, that's what you're going to have to do: fight fire with fire.

CONCLUSION

The Evil of the Ivory Tower

Pippin: "We don't belong here, Merry. It's too big for
us. What can we do in the end? We've got the Shire.
Maybe we should go home."
Merry: "The fires of Isengard will spread, and the
woods of Tuckborough and Buckland will burn. And
all that was once green and good in this world will be
gone. There won't be a Shire, Pippin."

—*The Lord of the Rings: The Two Towers*

College is sick. Academia is indoctrination. The ivory tower is corrupt. And we, the people, can no longer afford to treat that corruption as if it is someone else's problem. *It's ours. It is spreading through our society.* What happens on college campuses spreads into institutions and into our streets. It is "cancel culture." It is the degrading of Western civilization. It is the affirmation of leftist racism and violence. It is the insanity of LGBTQ+.

If you want to know what is in store for society if this goes unchecked, just look at what is happening in our colleges and universities. For every item listed below, there are hundreds, if not thousands, of others. We've grown too used to this sort of behavior. For instance,

- In 2016, Hampshire College removed all of its American flags on campus after "students pulled down the flag the night before Veteran's Day and set it on fire." As a direct consequence of this act, the president of Hampshire College announced, "Henceforth, no American flags will be flown on campus. Getting rid of the flag will enable us to instead focus our efforts on addressing racist, misogynistic, Islamophobic, anti-immigrant, anti-Semitic, and anti-LGBTQ rhetoric and behaviors."[1]

- On September 26, 2016, at Reed College, "more than 400 marching 'Reedies Against Racism' boycotted classes" and "briefly disrupted" Reed's Humanities 110 lecture, its famous Western civilization requirement for entering freshman. "Two days later protesting students began surrounding the Hum 110 lecturer on stage during each class session."[2] Caving to the mob pressure, in 2018 Reed officially announced it would be majorly overhauling the content of the Humanities 110 requirement.[3]

- In 2017, with the intent of phasing out the "'oppressive' gender binary, the University of Nebraska-Omaha has provided its students with a handy guide to 'queer and trans community language.' The glossary includes a 'Gender Unicorn' worksheet that students can use to determine exactly where they fit on the gender-identity spectrum."[4]

- In 2017, the University of California, Davis published "a glossary of popular social-justice themed terms...that plainly asserts that only white people are capable of racism."[5]

- In March 2017, at Middlebury College, Professor Allison Stanger was hospitalized for whiplash after an angry student protestor yanked on the back of her hair as she and Charles Murray, a campus speaker and author of *The Bell Curve*, fled to her car after being rushed by a violent group of student protestors.[6]

- In spring 2017, at Evergreen State College, professor of evolutionary biology Brett Weinstein inadvertently garnered the ire of a student mob hellbent on pressuring all white students and faculty to leave the campus during Evergreen's annual "Day of Absence." Campus police cautioned Weinstein that gangs of students were roving the campus brandishing baseball bats looking for him and his wife, fellow professor Heather Heying. In the aftermath, he and his wife resigned their positions at the college.[7]

- In December 2017, Drexel professor of political science, George Ciccariello-Maher, posted on Twitter that "All I want for Christmas is white genocide."[8]

- In 2017, the University of Maryland began instructing students to "avoid terms with 'man' in them, such as 'freshman' and 'chairman'" because such phrasing supposedly suggests that "women cannot perform in these roles."[9]

- In 2017, the University of Dayton "provided its students with a guide on 'gender neutral language,' saying phrases like 'gentlemen's agreement' should be replaced with 'informal agreement'" or 'contract' while 'spouse, partner, [and] significant other' should be used instead of 'husband' and 'wife.'"[10]

- In 2017, at Bethel University, administrators encouraged faculty-members "'to be clear in our Christian witness' by eschewing masculine terminology, despite the Bible consistently referring to humans as 'man' or 'mankind.'"[11]

- In April 2018, Eric Clanton, professor of ethics at Diablo State Community College in California, was recorded on camera clad in an all-black uniform and black ski mask, assaulting seven Trump supporters with a U-shaped bike lock, leaving one of his victims with a major laceration in his head requiring five staples. For his unorthodox teaching methods, four felony assault charges, and use of his bike-lock-of-tolerance to open minds, Clanton garnered a sentence of three-year probation.[12]

- In 2018, at Queen's University in Ontario, during a speech delivered by best-selling author and free-speech advocate Dr. Jordan Peterson, a mob of dozens of students pounded on the "stained glass windows of the historic Victorian Romanesque-style building" within which the speech was being given, breaking one of the windows. The mob then "blocked the front and back doors of the hall with trash and recycling bins" while one woman yelled, "Lock them in and burn it down!" "to the cheers of the other protestors." Eventually, "police were called to the scene."[13]

- In February 2019, a conservative student activist was assaulted at Sproul Plaza at the University of California Berkeley, the supposed "birthplace" of the 1960s free-speech movement. The victim, Hayden Williams, wrote in *USA TODAY*, "I've seen the intolerance and hate toward conservatives on our campuses with my own eyes, and the only difference between what happened to me on Feb. 19 and every other day is that the event was caught on video. Conservative students across the country have suffered verbal and physical assault, social ostracism and even academic persecution for voicing their opinions on political topics. This is because young liberals believe that they are on the morally righteous side in a culture war and, in order to win, they must silence any form of dissent. Leftists and the progressives aspire to nothing less than to make it de facto impossible to be conservative in public."[14]

- In 2019, at a Young America Foundation talk at the University of Missouri-Kansas City, conservative political commentator Michael Knowles "was attacked by a left-wing protester…for proclaiming that 'Men Are Not Women.'" He "was doused in a glitter-filled liquid after being repeatedly interrupted by shouting protestors for questioning transgenderism."[15]

- In 2019, the University of Kansas began offering an "Angry White Male Studies" course to evaluate "recent manifestations of male anger." The course, which requires as a prerequisite a course in "Women, Gender, and Sexuality," is explained thus: "Employing interdisciplinary perspectives this course examines how both dominant and subordinate masculinities are represented and experienced in cultures undergoing periods of rapid change connected to modernity as well as to rights-based movements of women, people of color, homosexuals and trans individuals."[16]

- In June 2020, in the wake of the George Floyd riots, student and professor activists at the University of Southern Maine "strongly encouraged" fellow community members to sign a Black Lives Matter "anti-racism pledge" and to keep track of all students and professors who did not sign the pledge.[17]

- In December 2020, University of Sussex professor of philosophy Kathleen Stock was appointed Officer of the Order of the British Empire. Shortly thereafter, a group of six hundred academics criticized her official appointment, arguing that Stock's previous writings and statements critiquing transgenderism constituted "harmful rhetoric" contributing to the marginalization of transgender people. In October 2021, Stock resigned from the university after a student campaign calling for her dismissal and accusing the university of "institutional transphobia."[18]

- In July 2021, the front page of the London School of Economics Gender Studies Department website posted grad student Matt Thomson's claim that "if TERFs [trans-exclusionary radical feminists] think trans* is an endemic threat to feminism, let us be the threat to feminism. . . . Picture this: I hold a knife to your throat and spit my transness into your ear. Does that turn you on? Are you scared? I sure fucking hope so."[19]

- In fall 2021, University of Pennsylvania "transfemale" swimmer Lia Thomas won the women's 1650-yard freestyle, shattering the national college record by more than 38 seconds, and won three other women's events that same weekend.[20]

- In October 2021, Brittney Cooper, a professor of Women's and Gender Studies and Africana Studies at Rutgers University, celebrated the decline of white birth-rates in America, calling white people "villains," and stating that "we need to take the motherfuckers out!"[21]

- In February 2022, "former UCLA 'Philosophy of Race' lecturer Matthew Harris was arrested for threatening to commit a mass shooting against white members of the UCLA Philosophy department."[22]

If you are a student—we say *don't go to college.* Don't incur the debt, don't subject yourself to the indoctrination, don't waste your time—and don't waste your life. If you are an adult—especially if you are a private college alumnus, or an elected official, or a beleaguered conservative college administrator or professor—we demand that you step up and do your part. Dismantle the money-sucking, soul-destroying, poisonous institution that the ivory tower has become. In its place, restore the sanity and beauty, the faith and culture, the truth and honest patriotism that will come with a return to the classic Aristotelian-Scholastic model of higher education. That was the very same model that made American and Western civilization flourish. We had it once. We can have it again. But only if we first overthrow the insane woke tyranny of the ivory tower.

Après la Révolution: Cardinal Newman on Restoring the Idea of a University

No one wrote more brilliantly on the idea of a university than John Henry Cardinal Newman. Indeed, his book with that title, *The Idea of a University*, remains the classic definition of what a university should be. Once our current corrupt system of higher education is overthrown, and it will be, his treatise—which covers all aspects of higher education, from the liberal arts to the sciences—should be the guidebook for what replaces it. In the brief space we have here, we reproduce its preface, introductory discourse, and discourse on "knowledge its own end."

He speaks of a Catholic university, and, as we have pointed out, it was the Catholic Church that founded the first universities, proper universities, with natural law at their center—and that is the model we should follow. Newman not only puts a university education in its rightful sphere, he knows what the ultimate stakes are, and here he gets the final word:

If the powers of intellect decay, the powers of the body have
decayed before them, and, as an Hospital or an Almshouse,
though its end be ephemeral, may be sanctified to the service of religion, so surely may a University, even were it
nothing more than I have as yet described it. We attain to
heaven by using this world well, though it is to pass away;
we perfect our nature, not by undoing it, but by adding to
it what is more than nature, and directing it towards aims
higher than its own.

Preface

THE view taken of a University in these Discourses is the following:—That it is a place of *teaching* universal *knowledge*. This
implies that its object is, on the one hand, intellectual, not moral; and,
on the other, that it is the diffusion and extension of knowledge rather
than the advancement. If its object were scientific and philosophical
discovery, I do not see why a University should have students; if religious training, I do not see how it can be the seat of literature and
science.

Such is a University in its *essence*, and independently of its relation
to the Church. But, practically speaking, it cannot fulfil its object duly,
such as I have described it, without the Church's assistance; or, to use
the theological term, the Church is necessary for its *integrity*. Not that
its main characters are changed by this incorporation: it still has the
office of intellectual education; but the Church steadies it in the performance of that office.

Such are the main principles of the Discourses which follow;
though it would be unreasonable for me to expect that I have treated
so large and important a field of thought with the fulness and preci-
sion necessary to secure me from incidental misconceptions of my

meaning on the part of the reader. It is true, there is nothing novel or singular in the argument which I have been pursuing, but this does not protect me from such misconceptions; for the very circumstance that the views I have been delineating are not original with me may lead to false notions as to my relations in opinion towards those from whom I happened in the first instance to learn them, and may cause me to be interpreted by the objects or sentiments of schools to which I should be simply opposed.

For instance, some persons may be tempted to complain, that I have servilely followed the English idea of a University, to the disparagement of that Knowledge which I profess to be so strenuously upholding; and they may anticipate that an academical system, formed upon my model, will result in nothing better or higher than in the production of that antiquated variety of human nature and remnant of feudalism, as they consider it, called "a gentleman." [Note 1] Now, I have anticipated this charge in various parts of my discussion; if, however, any Catholic is found to prefer it (and to Catholics of course this Volume is primarily addressed), I would have him first of all ask himself the previous question, *what* he conceives to be the reason contemplated by the Holy See in recommending just now to the Irish Hierarchy the establishment of a Catholic University? Has the Supreme Pontiff recommended it for the sake of the Sciences, which are to be the matter, and not rather of the Students, who are to be the subjects, of its teaching? Has he any obligation or duty at all towards secular knowledge as such? Would it become his Apostolical Ministry, and his descent from the Fisherman, to have a zeal for the Baconian or other philosophy of man for its own sake? Is the Vicar of Christ bound by office or by vow to be the preacher of the theory of gravitation, or a martyr for electro-magnetism? Would he be acquitting himself of the dispensation committed to him if he were smitten with an abstract love of these matters, however true, or beautiful, or ingenious, or useful? Or rather, does he not contemplate such achievements of the intellect, as far as he contemplates them, solely and simply in their relation to the interests of Revealed Truth? Surely, what he does he does for the sake of Religion; if he looks with satisfaction on strong temporal governments, which promise perpetuity, it is for the sake of Religion; and if he encourages and patronizes art and science, it is for the sake of Religion. He rejoices in the widest and most philosophical systems of intellectual education, from an intimate conviction that Truth is his real ally, as it is his profession; and that Knowledge and Reason are sure ministers to Faith.

This being undeniable, it is plain that, when he suggests to the Irish Hierarchy the establishment of a University, his first and chief and direct object is, not science, art, professional skill, literature, the discovery of knowledge, but some benefit or other, to accrue, by means of literature and science, to his own children; not indeed their formation on any narrow or fantastic type, as, for instance, that of an "English Gentleman" may be called, but their exercise and growth in certain habits, moral or intellectual. Nothing short of this can be his aim, if, as becomes the Successor of the Apostles, he is to be able to say with St. Paul, "Non judicavi me scire aliquid inter vos, nisi Jesum Christum, et hunc crucifixum." Just as a commander wishes to have tall and well-formed and vigorous soldiers, not from any abstract devotion to the military standard of height or age, but for the purposes of war, and no one thinks it any thing but natural and praiseworthy in him to be contemplating, not abstract qualities, but his own living and breathing men; so, in like manner, when the Church founds a University, she is not cherishing talent, genius, or knowledge, for their own sake, but for the sake of her children, with a view to their spiritual welfare and their religious influence and usefulness, with the object of training them to fill their respective posts in life better, and of making them more intelligent, capable, active members of society.

Nor can it justly be said that in thus acting she sacrifices Science, and, under a pretence of fulfilling the duties of her mission, perverts a University to ends not its own, as soon as it is taken into account that there are other institutions far more suited to act as instruments of stimulating philosophical inquiry, and extending the boundaries of our knowledge, than a University. Such, for instance, are the literary and scientific "Academies," which are so celebrated in Italy and France, and which have frequently been connected with Universities, as committees, or, as it were, congregations or delegacies subordinate to them. Thus the present Royal Society originated in Charles the Second's time, in Oxford; such just now are the Ashmolean and Architectural Societies in the same seat of learning, which have risen in our own time. Such, too, is the British Association, a migratory body, which at least at times is found in the halls of the Protestant Universities of the United Kingdom, and the faults of which lie, not in its exclusive devotion to science, but in graver matters which it is irrelevant here to enter upon. Such again is the Antiquarian Society, the Royal Academy for the Fine Arts, and others which might be mentioned. This, then, is the sort of institution, which primarily contemplates Science itself; and not students: and, in thus speaking, I am saying nothing of my own, being supported by no less an authority than Cardinal Gerdil. "Ce n'est pas," he says, "qu'il y ait aucune véritable opposition entre l'esprit des Académies et celui des Universités; ce sont seulement des vues différentes. Les Universités sont établies pour *enseigner* les sciences *aux élèves* qui veulent s'y former; les Académies se proposent *de nouvelles recherches* à faire dans la carrière des sciences. Les Universités d'Italie ont fourni des sujets qui ont fait honneur aux Académies; et celles-ci ont donné aux

Universités des Professeurs, qui out rempli les chaires avec la plus grande distinction." [Note 2]

The nature of the case and the history of philosophy combine to recommend to us this division of intellectual labour between Academies and Universities. To discover and to teach are distinct functions; they are also distinct gifts, and are not commonly found united in the same person. He, too, who spends his day in dispensing his existing knowledge to all comers is unlikely to have either leisure or energy to acquire new. The common sense of mankind has associated the search after truth with seclusion and quiet. The greatest thinkers have been too intent on their subject to admit of interruption; they have been men of absent minds and idiosyncratic habits, and have, more or less, shunned the lecture room and the public school. Pythagoras, the light of Magna Græcia, lived for a time in a cave. Thales, the light of Ionia, lived unmarried and in private, and refused the invitations of princes. Plato withdrew from Athens to the groves of Academus. Aristotle gave twenty years to a studious discipleship under him. Friar Bacon lived in his tower upon the Isis. Newton indulged in an intense severity of meditation which almost shook his reason. The great discoveries in chemistry and electricity were not made in Universities. Observatories are more frequently out of Universities than in them, and even when within their bounds need have no moral connexion with them. Porson had no classes; Elmsley lived good part of his life in the country. I do not say that there are not great examples the other way, perhaps Socrates, certainly Lord Bacon; still I think it must be allowed on the whole that, while teaching involves external engagements, the natural home for experiment and speculation is retirement.

Returning, then, to the consideration of the question, from which I may seem to have digressed, thus much I think I have made good,— that, whether or no a Catholic University should put before it, as its great object, to make its students "gentlemen," still to make them something or other is its great object, and not simply to protect the interests and advance the dominion of Science. If, then, this may be taken for granted, as I think it may, the only point which remains to be settled is, whether I have formed a probable conception of the *sort of benefit* which the Holy See has intended to confer on Catholics who speak the English tongue by recommending to the Irish Hierarchy the establishment of a University; and this I now proceed to consider.

Here, then, it is natural to ask those who are interested in the question, whether any better interpretation of the recommendation of the Holy See can be given than that which I have suggested in this Volume. Certainly it does not seem to me rash to pronounce that, whereas Protestants have great advantages of education in the Schools, Colleges, and Universities of the United Kingdom, our ecclesiastical rulers have it in purpose that Catholics should enjoy the like advantages, whatever they are, to the full. I conceive they view it as prejudicial to the interests of Religion that there should be any cultivation of mind bestowed upon Protestants which is not given to their own youth also. As they wish their schools for the poorer and middle classes to be at least on a par with those of Protestants, they contemplate the same object also as regards that higher education which is given to comparatively the few. Protestant youths, who can spare the time, continue their studies till the age of twenty-one or twenty-two; thus they employ a time of life all-important and especially favourable to mental culture. I conceive that our Prelates are impressed with the fact and its consequences, that a youth who ends his education at seventeen is no match (*cæteris paribus*) for one who ends it at twenty-two.

All classes indeed of the community are impressed with a fact so obvious as this. The consequence is, that Catholics who aspire to be on a level with Protestants in discipline and refinement of intellect have recourse to Protestant Universities to obtain what they cannot find at home. Assuming (as the Rescripts from Propaganda allow me to do) that Protestant education is inexpedient for our youth,—we see here an additional reason why those advantages, whatever they are, which Protestant communities dispense through the medium of Protestantism should be accessible to Catholics in a Catholic form.

What are these advantages? I repeat, they are in one word the culture of the intellect. Robbed, oppressed, and thrust aside, Catholics in these islands have not been in a condition for centuries to attempt the sort of education which is necessary for the man of the world, the statesman, the landholder, or the opulent gentleman. Their legitimate stations, duties, employments, have been taken from them, and the qualifications withal, social and intellectual, which are necessary both for reversing the forfeiture and for availing themselves of the reversal. The time is come when this moral disability must be removed. Our desideratum is, not the manners and habits of gentlemen;—these can be, and are, acquired in various other ways, by good society, by foreign travel, by the innate grace and dignity of the Catholic mind;—but the force, the steadiness, the comprehensiveness and the versatility of intellect, the command over our own powers, the instinctive just estimate of things as they pass before us, which sometimes indeed is a natural gift, but commonly is not gained without much effort and the exercise of years.

This is real cultivation of mind; and I do not deny that the characteristic excellences of a gentleman are included in it. Nor need we be ashamed that they should be, since the poet long ago wrote, that "Ingenuas didicisse fideliter artes Emollit mores." Certainly a liberal education does manifest itself in a courtesy, propriety, and polish of word and action, which is beautiful in itself, and acceptable to others; but it does much more. It brings the mind into form,—for the mind is like the body. Boys outgrow their shape and their strength; their limbs have to be knit together, and their constitution needs tone. Mistaking animal spirits for vigour, and overconfident in their health, ignorant what they can bear and how to manage themselves, they are immoderate and extravagant; and fall into sharp sicknesses. This is an emblem of their minds; at first they have no principles laid down within them as a foundation for the intellect to build upon; they have no discriminating convictions, and no grasp of consequences. And therefore they talk at random, if they talk much, and cannot help being flippant, or what is emphatically called "*young.*" They are merely dazzled by phenomena, instead of perceiving things as they are.

It were well if none remained boys all their lives; but what more common than the sight of grown men, talking on political or moral or religious subjects, in that offhand, idle way, which we signify by the word *unreal*? "That they simply do not know what they are talking about" is the spontaneous silent remark of any man of sense who hears them. Hence such persons have no difficulty in contradicting themselves in successive sentences, without being conscious of it. Hence others, whose defect in intellectual training is more latent, have their most unfortunate crotchets, as they are called, or hobbies, which deprive them of the influence which their estimable qualities would otherwise secure. Hence others can never look straight before them, never see the point, and have no difficulties in the most difficult subjects. Others are hopelessly obstinate and prejudiced, and, after they have been driven from their opinions, return to them the next moment without even an attempt to explain why. Others are so intemperate and intractable that there is no greater calamity for a good cause than that they should get hold of it. It is very plain from the very particulars I have mentioned that, in this delineation of intellectual infirmities, I am drawing, not from Catholics, but from the world at large; I am referring to an evil which is forced upon us in every railway carriage, in every coffee-room or *table-d'hôte*, in every mixed company, an evil, however, to which Catholics are not less exposed than the rest of mankind.

When the intellect has once been properly trained and formed to have a connected view or grasp of things, it will display its powers with more or less effect according to its particular quality and capacity in the individual. In the case of most men it makes itself felt in the good sense, sobriety of thought, reasonableness, candour, self-command, and steadiness of view, which characterize it. In some it will have developed habits of business, power of influencing others, and sagacity. In others it will elicit the talent of philosophical speculation, and lead the mind forward to eminence in this or that intellectual department. In all it will be a faculty of entering with comparative ease into any subject of thought, and of taking up with aptitude any science or profession. All this it will be and will do in a measure, even when the mental formation be made after a model but partially true; for, as far as effectiveness goes, even false views of things have more influence and inspire more respect than no views at all. Men who fancy they see what is not are more energetic, and make their way better, than those who see nothing; and so the undoubting infidel, the fanatic, the heresiarch, are able to do much, while the mere hereditary Christian, who has never realized the truths which he holds, is unable to do any thing. But, if consistency of view can add so much strength even to error, what may it not be expected to furnish to the dignity, the energy, and the influence of Truth!

Some one, however, will perhaps object that I am but advocating that spurious philosophism, which shows itself in what, for want of a word, I may call "viewiness," when I speak so much of the formation, and consequent grasp, of the intellect. It may be said that the theory of University Education, which I have been delineating, if acted upon, would teach youths nothing soundly or thoroughly, and would dismiss them with nothing better than brilliant general views about all things whatever.

This indeed, if well founded, would be a most serious objection to what I have advanced in this Volume, and would demand my immediate attention, had I any reason to think that I could not remove it at once, by a simple explanation of what I consider the true *mode* of educating, were this the place to do so. But these Discourses are directed simply to the consideration of the *aims* and *principles* of Education. Suffice it, then, to say here, that I hold very strongly that the first step in intellectual training is to impress upon a boy's mind the idea of science, method, order, principle, and system; of rule and exception, of richness and harmony. This is commonly and excellently done by making him begin with Grammar; nor can too great accuracy, or minuteness and subtlety of teaching be used towards him, as his faculties expand, with this simple purpose. Hence it is that critical scholarship is so important a discipline for him when he is leaving school for the University. A second science is the Mathematics: this should follow Grammar, still with the same object, viz., to give him a conception of development and arrangement from and around a common centre. Hence it is that Chronology and Geography are so necessary for him, when he reads History, which is otherwise little better than a storybook. Hence, too, Metrical Composition, when he reads Poetry; in order to stimulate his powers into action in every practicable way, and to prevent a merely passive reception of images and ideas which in that case are likely to pass out of the mind as soon as they have entered it. Let him once gain this habit of method, of starting from fixed points, of making his ground good as he goes, of distinguishing what he knows from what he does not know, and I conceive he will be gradually initiated into the largest and truest philosophical views, and will feel nothing but impatience and disgust at the random theories and imposing sophistries and dashing paradoxes, which carry away half-formed and superficial intellects.

Such parti-coloured ingenuities are indeed one of the chief evils of the day, and men of real talent are not slow to minister to them. An intellectual man, as the world now conceives of him, is one who is full of "views" on all subjects of philosophy, on all matters of the day. It is almost thought a disgrace not to have a view at a moment's notice on any question from the Personal Advent to the Cholera or Mesmerism. This is owing in great measure to the necessities of periodical literature, now so much in request. Every quarter of a year, every month, every day, there must be a supply, for the gratification of the public, of new and luminous theories on the subjects of religion, foreign politics, home politics, civil economy, finance, trade, agriculture, emigration, and the colonies. Slavery, the gold fields, German philosophy, the French Empire, Wellington, Peel, Ireland, must all be practised on, day after day, by what are called original thinkers. As the great man's guest must produce his good stories or songs at the evening banquet, as the platform orator exhibits his telling facts at mid-day, so the journalist lies under the stern obligation of extemporizing his lucid views, leading ideas, and nutshell truths for the breakfast table. The very nature of periodical literature, broken into small wholes, and demanded punctually to an hour, involves the habit of this extempore philosophy. "Almost all the Ramblers," says Boswell of Johnson, "were written just as they were wanted for the press; he sent a certain portion of the copy of an essay, and wrote the remainder while the former part of it was printing." Few men have the gifts of Johnson, who to great vigour and resource of intellect, when it was fairly roused, united a rare common-sense and a conscientious regard for veracity, which preserved him from flippancy or extravagance in writing. Few men are Johnsons; yet how many men at this day are assailed by incessant demands on their mental powers, which only a productiveness like his could suitably supply! There is a demand for a reckless originality of thought, and a sparkling plausibility of argument, which he would have despised, even if he could have displayed; a demand for crude theory and unsound philosophy, rather than none at all. It is a sort of repetition of the "Quid novi?" of the Areopagus and it must have an answer. Men must be found who can treat, where it is necessary, like the Athenian sophist, *de omni scibili,*

> "Grammaticus, Rhetor, Geometres, Pictor, Aliptes,
> Augur, Schœnobates, Medicus, Magus, omnia novit."

I am speaking of such writers with a feeling of real sympathy for men who are under the rod of a cruel slavery. I have never indeed been in such circumstances myself nor in the temptations which they involve; but most men who have had to do with composition must know the distress which at times it occasions them to have to write—a distress sometimes so keen and so specific that it resembles nothing else than bodily pain. That pain is the token of the wear and tear of mind; and, if works done comparatively at leisure involve such mental fatigue and exhaustion, what must be the toil of those whose intellects are to be flaunted daily before the public in full dress, and that dress ever new and varied, and spun, like the silkworm's, out of themselves! Still, whatever true sympathy we may feel for the ministers of this dearly purchased luxury, and whatever sense we may have of the great intellectual power which the literature in question displays, we cannot honestly close our eyes to its direct evil.

One other remark suggests itself, which is the last I shall think it necessary to make. The authority, which in former times was lodged in Universities, now resides in very great measure in that literary world, as it is called, to which I have been referring. This is not satisfactory, if, as no one can deny, its teaching be so offhand, so ambitious, so changeable. It increases the seriousness of the mischief, that so very large a portion of its writers are anonymous, for irresponsible power never can be any thing but a great evil; and, moreover, that, even when they are known, they can give no better guarantee for the philosophical truth of their principles than their popularity at the moment, and their happy conformity in ethical character to the age which admires them. Protestants, however, may do as they will: it is a matter for their own consideration; but at least it concerns us that our own literary tribunals and oracles of moral duty should bear a graver character. At least it is a matter of deep solicitude to Catholic Prelates that their people should be taught a wisdom, safe from the excesses and vagaries of individuals, embodied in institutions which have stood the trial and received the sanction of ages, and administered by men who have no need to be anonymous, as being supported by their consistency with their predecessors and with each other.

John Henry Cardinal Newman
November 21, 1852

Notes

1.   *Vid.* Huber's English Universities, London, 1843, vol. ii., part I., pp. 321, etc.

2.   Opere, t. iii., p. 353.

Discourse 1: Introductory

IN addressing myself, Gentlemen, to the consideration of a question which has excited so much interest, and elicited so much discussion at the present day, as that of University Education, I feel some explanation is due from me for supposing, after such high ability and wide experience have been brought to bear upon it, that any field remains for the additional labours either of a disputant or of an inquirer. If, nevertheless, I still venture to ask permission to continue the discussion, already so protracted, it is because the subject of Liberal Education, and of the principles on which it must be conducted, has ever had a hold upon my own mind; and because I have lived the greater part of my life in a place which has all that time been occupied in a series of controversies both domestic and with strangers, and of measures, experimental or definitive, bearing upon it. About fifty years since, the English University, of which I was so long a member, after a century of inactivity, at length was roused, at a time when (as I may say) it was giving no education at all to the youth committed to its keeping, to a sense of the responsibilities which its profession and its station involved, and it presents to us the singular example of an heterogeneous and an independent body of men, setting about a work of self-reformation, not from any pressure of public opinion, but because it was fitting and right to undertake it. Its initial efforts, begun and carried on amid many obstacles, were met from without, as often happens in such cases, by ungenerous and jealous criticisms, which, at the very moment that they were urged, were beginning to be unjust. Controversy did but bring out more clearly to its own apprehension the views on which its reformation was proceeding, and throw them into a philosophical form. The course of beneficial change made progress, and what was at first but the result of individual energy and an act of the academical corporation, gradually became popular, and was taken up and carried out by the separate collegiate bodies, of which the University is composed. This was the first stage of the controversy. Years passed away, and then political adversaries arose against it, and the system of education which it had established was a second time assailed; but still, since that contest was conducted for the most part through the medium, not of political acts,

but of treatises and pamphlets, it happened as before that the threatened dangers, in the course of their repulse, did but afford fuller
development and more exact delineation to the principles of which
the University was the representative.

In the former of these two controversies the charge brought against
its studies was their remoteness from the occupations and duties of
life, to which they are the formal introduction, or, in other words, their
inutility; in the latter, it was their connexion with a particular form of
belief, or, in other words, their *religious exclusiveness*.

Living then so long as a witness, though hardly as an actor, in
these scenes of intellectual conflict, I am able to bear witness to views
of University Education, without authority indeed in themselves, but
not without value to a Catholic, and less familiar to him, as I conceive,
than they deserve to be. And, while an argument originating in the
controversies to which I have referred, may be serviceable at this
season to that great cause in which we are here so especially interested,
to me personally it will afford satisfaction of a peculiar kind; for,
though it has been my lot for many years to take a prominent, sometimes a presumptuous, part in theological discussions, yet the natural
turn of my mind carries me off to trains of thought like those which
I am now about to open, which, important though they be for Catholic
objects, and admitting of a Catholic treatment, are sheltered from the
extreme delicacy and peril which attach to disputations directly
bearing on the subject-matter of Divine Revelation.

There are several reasons why I should open the discussion with a
reference to the lessons with which past years have supplied me. One
reason is this: It would concern me, Gentlemen, were I supposed to have
got up my opinions for the occasion. This, indeed, would have been no
reflection on me personally, supposing I were persuaded of their truth,
when at length addressing myself to the inquiry; but it would have
destroyed, of course, the force of my testimony, and deprived such

arguments, as I might adduce, of that moral persuasiveness which attends on tried and sustained conviction. It would have made me seem the advocate, rather than the cordial and deliberate maintainer and witness, of the doctrines which I was to support; and, though it might be said to evidence the faith I reposed in the practical judgment of the Church, and the intimate concurrence of my own reason with the course she had authoritatively sanctioned, and the devotion with which I could promptly put myself at her disposal, it would have cast suspicion on the validity of reasonings and conclusions which rested on no independent inquiry, and appealed to no past experience. In that case it might have been plausibly objected by opponents that I was the serviceable expedient of an emergency, and never, after all, could be more than ingenious and adroit in the management of an argument which was not my own, and which I was sure to forget again as readily as I had mastered it. But this is not so. The views to which I have referred have grown into my whole system of thought, and are, as it were, part of myself. Many changes has my mind gone through: here it has known no variation or vacillation of opinion, and though this by itself is no proof of the truth of my principles, it puts a seal upon conviction, and is a justification of earnestness and zeal. Those principles, which I am now to set forth under the sanction of the Catholic Church, were my profession at that early period of my life, when religion was to me more a matter of feeling and experience than of faith. They did but take greater hold upon me, as I was introduced to the records of Christian Antiquity, and approached in sentiment and desire to Catholicism; and my sense of their correctness has been increased with the events of every year since I have been brought within its pale.

And here I am brought to a second and more important reason for referring, on this occasion, to the conclusions at which Protestants have arrived on the subject of Liberal Education; and it is as follows: Let it be observed, then, that the principles on which I would conduct the inquiry are attainable, as I have already implied, by the mere experience of life. They do not come simply of theology; they imply no supernatural discernment; they have no special connexion with Revelation; they almost arise out of the nature of the case; they are dictated even by human prudence and wisdom, though a divine illumination be absent, and they are recognized by common sense, even where self-interest is not present to quicken it; and, therefore, though true, and just, and good in themselves, they imply nothing whatever as to the religious profession of those who maintain them. They may be held by Protestants as well as by Catholics; nay, there is reason to anticipate that in certain times and places they will be more thoroughly investigated, and better understood, and held more firmly by Protestants than by ourselves.

It is natural to expect this from the very circumstance that the philosophy of Education is founded on truths in the natural order. Where the sun shines bright, in the warm climate of the south, the natives of the place know little of safeguards against cold and wet. They have, indeed, bleak and piercing blasts; they have chill and pouring rain, but only now and then, for a day or a week; they bear the inconvenience as they best may, but they have not made it an art to repel it; it is not worth their while; the science of calefaction and ventilation is reserved for the north. It is in this way that Catholics stand relatively to Protestants in the science of Education; Protestants depending on human means mainly, are led to make the most of them: their sole resource is to use what they have; "Knowledge is" their "power" and nothing else; they are the anxious cultivators of a rugged soil. It is otherwise with us; "*funes ceciderunt mihi in præclaris.*" We have a goodly inheritance. This is apt to cause us—I do not mean to rely too much on prayer, and the Divine Blessing, for that is impossible, but we sometimes forget that we shall please Him best, and get most from Him, when, according to the Fable, we "put our shoulder to the wheel," when we use what we have by nature to the utmost, at the same time that we look out for what is beyond nature in the confidence of faith and hope. However, we are sometimes tempted to let things take their course, as if they would in one way or another turn up right at last for certain; and so we go on, living from hand to mouth, getting into difficulties and getting out of them, succeeding certainly on the whole, but with failure in detail which might be avoided, and with much of imperfection or inferiority in our appointments and plans, and much disappointment, discouragement, and collision of opinion in consequence. If this be in any measure the state of the case, there is certainly so far a reason for availing ourselves of the investigations and experience of those who are not Catholics, when we have to address ourselves to the subject of Liberal Education.

Nor is there surely any thing derogatory to the position of a Catholic in such a proceeding. The Church has ever appealed and deferred to witnesses and authorities external to herself, in those matters in which she thought they had means of forming a judgment: and that on the principle, *Cuique in arte sua credendum.* She has even used unbelievers and pagans in evidence of her truth, as far as their testimony went. She avails herself of scholars, critics, and antiquarians, who are not of her communion. She has worded her theological teaching in the phraseology of Aristotle; Aquila, Symmachus, Theodotion, Origen, Eusebius, and Apollinaris, all more or less heterodox, have supplied materials for primitive exegetics. St. Cyprian called Tertullian his master; St. Augustin refers to Ticonius; Bossuet, in modern times, complimented the labours of the Anglican Bull; the Benedictine editors of the Fathers are familiar with the labours of Fell, Ussher, Pearson, and Beveridge. Pope Benedict XIV cites according to the occasion the works of Protestants without reserve, and the late French collection of Christian Apologists contains the writings of Locke, Burnet, Tillotson, and Paley. If, then, I come forward in any degree as borrowing the views of certain Protestant schools on the point which is to be discussed, I do so, Gentlemen, as believing, first, that the Catholic Church has ever, in the plenitude of her divine illumination, made use of whatever truth or wisdom she has found in their teaching or their measures; and next, that in particular places or times her children are likely to profit from external suggestions or lessons, which have not been provided for them by herself.

And here I may mention a third reason for appealing at the outset to the proceedings of Protestant bodies in regard to Liberal Education. It will serve to intimate the mode in which I propose to handle my subject altogether. Observe then, Gentlemen, I have no intention, in any thing I shall say, of bringing into the argument the authority of the Church, or any authority at all; but I shall consider the question simply on the grounds of human reason and human wisdom. I am investigating in the abstract, and am determining what is in itself right and true. For the moment I know nothing, so to say, of history. I take things as I find them; I have no concern with the past; I find myself here; I set myself to the duties I find here; I set myself to further, by every means in my power, doctrines and views, true in themselves, recognized by Catholics as such, familiar to my own mind; and to do this quite apart from the consideration of questions which have been determined without me and before me. I am here the advocate and the minister of a certain great principle; yet not merely advocate and minister, else had I not been here at all. It has been my previous keen sense and hearty reception of that principle, that has been at once the reason, as I must suppose, of my being selected for this office, and is the cause of my accepting it. I am told on authority that a principle is expedient, which I have ever felt to be true. And I argue in its behalf on its own merits, the authority, which brings me here, being my opportunity for arguing, but not the ground of my argument itself.

And a fourth reason is here suggested for consulting the history of Protestant institutions, when I am going to speak of the object and nature of University Education. It will serve to remind you, Gentlemen, that I am concerned with questions, not simply of immutable truth, but of practice and expedience. It would ill have become me to undertake a subject, on which points of dispute have arisen among persons so far above me in authority and name, in relation to a state of society, about which I have so much to learn, if it involved an appeal to sacred truths, or the determination of some imperative rule of conduct. It would have been presumptuous in me so to have acted, nor am I so acting. Even the question of the union of Theology with the secular Sciences, which is its religious side, simple as it is of solution in the abstract, has, according to difference of circumstances, been at different times differently decided. Necessity has no law, and expedience is often one form of necessity. It is no principle with sensible men, of whatever cast of opinion, to do always what is abstractedly best. Where no direct duty forbids, we may be obliged to do, as being best under circumstances, what we murmur and rise against, while we do it. We see that to attempt more is to effect less; that we must accept so much, or gain nothing; and so perforce we reconcile ourselves to what we would have far otherwise, if we could. Thus a system of what is called secular Education, in which Theology and the Sciences are taught separately, may, in a particular place or time, be the least of evils; it may be of long standing; it may be dangerous to meddle with; it may be professedly a temporary arrangement; it may be under a process of improvement; its disadvantages may be neutralized by the persons by whom, or the provisions under which, it is administered.

Hence it was, that in the early ages the Church allowed her children to attend the heathen schools for the acquisition of secular accomplishments, where, as no one can doubt, evils existed, at least as great as can attend on Mixed Education now. The gravest Fathers recommended for Christian youth the use of Pagan masters; the most saintly Bishops and most authoritative Doctors had been sent in their adolescence by Christian parents to Pagan lecture halls [Note 1]. And, not to take other instances, at this very time, and in this very country, as regards at least the poorer classes of the community, whose secular acquirements ever must be limited, it has seemed best to the Irish Bishops, under the circumstances, to suffer the introduction into the country of a system of Mixed Education in the schools called National. Such a state of things, however, is passing away; as regards University education at least, the highest authority has now decided that the plan, which is abstractedly best, is in this time and country also most expedient.

And here I have an opportunity of recognizing once for all that higher view of approaching the subject of these Discourses, which, after this formal recognition, I mean to dispense with. Ecclesiastical authority, not argument, is the supreme rule and the appropriate guide for Catholics in matters of religion. It has always the right to interpose, and sometimes, in the conflict of parties and opinions, it is called on to exercise that right. It has lately exercised it in our own instance: it has interposed in favour of a pure University system for Catholic youth, forbidding compromise or accommodation of any kind. Of course its decision must be heartily accepted and obeyed, and that the more, because the decision proceeds, not simply from the Bishops of Ireland, great as their authority is, but the highest authority on earth, from the Chair of St. Peter.

Moreover, such a decision not only demands our submission, but has a claim upon our trust. It not only acts as a prohibition of any measures, but as an *ipso facto* confutation of any reasonings, inconsistent with it. It carries with it an earnest and an augury of its own expediency. For instance, I can fancy, Gentlemen, there may be some, among those who hear me, disposed to say that they are ready to acquit the principles of Education, which I am to advocate, of all fault whatever, except that of being impracticable. I can fancy them granting to me, that those principles are most correct and most obvious, simply irresistible on paper, but maintaining, nevertheless, that after all, they are nothing more than the dreams of men who live out of the world, and who do not see the difficulty of keeping Catholicism anyhow afloat on the bosom of this wonderful nineteenth century. Proved, indeed, those principles are, to demonstration, but they will not work. Nay, it was my own admission just now, that, in a particular instance, it might easily happen, that what is only second best is best practically, because what is actually best is out of the question.

This, I hear you say to yourselves, is the state of things at present. You recount in detail the numberless impediments, great and small, formidable or only vexatious, which at every step embarrass the attempt to carry out ever so poorly a principle in itself so true and ecclesiastical. You appeal in your defence to wise and sagacious intellects, who are far from enemies to Catholicism, or to the Irish Hierarchy, and you have no hope, or rather you absolutely disbelieve, that Education can possibly be conducted, here and now, on a theological principle, or that youths of different religions can, under the circumstances of the country, be educated apart from each other. The more you think over the state of politics, the position of parties, the feelings of classes, and the experience of the past, the more chimerical does it seem to you to aim at a University, of which Catholicity is the fundamental principle. Nay, even if the attempt could accidentally succeed, would not the mischief exceed the benefit of it? How great the sacrifices, in how many ways, by which it would be preceded and followed! how many wounds, open and secret, would it inflict upon the body politic! And, if it fails, which is to be expected, then a double mischief will ensue from its recognition of evils which it has been unable to remedy. These are your deep misgivings; and, in proportion to the force with which they come to you, is the concern and anxiety which you feel, that there should be those whom you love, whom you revere, who from one cause or other refuse to enter into them.

This, I repeat, is what some good Catholics will say to me, and more than this. They will express themselves better than I can speak for them in their behalf,—with more earnestness and point, with more force of argument and fulness of detail; and I will frankly and at once acknowledge, that I shall insist on the high theological view of a University without attempting to give a direct answer to their arguments against its present practicability. I do not say an answer cannot be given; on the contrary, I have a confident expectation that, in proportion as those objections are looked in the face, they will fade away. But, however this may be, it would not become me to argue the matter with those who understand the circumstances of the problem so much better than myself. What do I know of the state of things in Ireland, that I should presume to put ideas of mine, which could not be right except by accident, by the side of theirs, who speak in the country of their birth and their home? No, Gentlemen, you are natural judges of the difficulties which beset us, and they are doubtless greater than I can even fancy or forbode. Let me, for the sake of argument, admit all you say against our enterprise, and a great deal more. Your proof of its intrinsic impossibility shall be to me as cogent as my own of its theological advisableness. Why, then, should I be so rash and perverse as to involve myself in trouble not properly mine? Why go out of my own place? Why so headstrong and reckless as to lay up for myself miscarriage and disappointment, as though I were not sure to have enough of personal trial anyhow without going about to seek for it?

Reflections such as these would be decisive even with the boldest and most capable minds, but for one consideration. In the midst of our difficulties I have one ground of hope, just one stay, but, as I think, a sufficient one, which serves me in the stead of all other argument whatever, which hardens me against criticism, which supports me if I begin to despond, and to which I ever come round, when the question of the possible and the expedient is brought into discussion. It is the decision of the Holy See; St. Peter has spoken, it is he who has enjoined that which seems to us so unpromising. He has spoken, and has a claim on us to trust him. He is no recluse, no solitary student, no dreamer about the past, no doter upon the dead and gone, no projector of the visionary. He for eighteen hundred years has lived in the world; he has seen all fortunes, he has encountered all adversaries, he has shaped himself for all emergencies. If ever there was a power on earth who had an eye for the times, who has confined himself to the practicable, and has been happy in his anticipations, whose words have been facts, and whose commands prophecies, such is he in the history of ages, who sits from generation to generation in the Chair of the Apostles, as the Vicar of Christ, and the Doctor of His Church.

These are not the words of rhetoric, Gentlemen, but of history. All who take part with the Apostle, are on the winning side. He has long since given warrants for the confidence which he claims. From the first he has looked through the wide world, of which he has the burden; and, according to the need of the day, and the inspirations of his Lord, he has set himself now to one thing, now to another; but to all in season, and to nothing in vain. He came first upon an age of refinement and luxury like our own, and, in spite of the persecutor, fertile in the resources of his cruelty, he soon gathered, out of all classes of society, the slave, the soldier, the high-born lady, and the sophist, materials enough to form a people to his Master's honour. The savage hordes came down in torrents from the north, and Peter went out to meet them, and by his very eye he sobered them, and backed them in their full career. They turned aside and flooded the whole earth, but only to be more surely civilized by him, and to be made ten times more his children even than the older populations which they had overwhelmed. Lawless kings arose, sagacious as the Roman, passionate as the Hun, yet in him they found their match, and were shattered, and he lived on. The gates of the earth were opened to the east and west, and men poured out to take possession; but he went with them by his missionaries, to China, to Mexico, carried along by zeal and charity, as far as those children of men were led by enterprise, covetousness, or ambition. Has he failed in his successes up to this hour? Did he, in our fathers' day, fail in his struggle with Joseph of Germany and his confederates, with Napoleon, a greater name, and his dependent kings, that, though in another kind of fight, he should fail in ours? What grey hairs are on the head of Judah, whose youth is renewed like the eagle's, whose feet are like the feet of harts, and underneath the Everlasting arms?

In the first centuries of the Church all this practical sagacity of Holy Church was mere matter of faith, but every age, as it has come, has confirmed faith by actual sight; and shame on us, if, with the accumulated testimony of eighteen centuries, our eyes are too gross to see those victories which the Saints have ever seen by anticipation. Least of all can we, the Catholics of islands which have in the cultivation and diffusion of Knowledge heretofore been so singularly united under the auspices of the Apostolic See, least of all can we be the men to distrust its wisdom and to predict its failure, when it sends us on a similar mission now. I cannot forget that, at a time when Celt and Saxon were alike savage, it was the See of Peter that gave both of them, first faith, then civilization; and then again bound them together in one by the seal of a joint commission to convert and illuminate in their turn the pagan continent. I cannot forget how it was from Rome that the glorious St. Patrick was sent to Ireland, and did a work so great that he could not have a successor in it, the sanctity and learning and zeal and charity which followed on his death being but the result of the one impulse which he gave. I cannot forget how, in no long time, under the fostering breath of the Vicar of Christ, a country of heathen superstitions became the very wonder and asylum of all people,—the wonder by reason of its knowledge, sacred and profane, and the asylum of religion, literature and science, when chased away from the continent by the barbarian invaders. I recollect its hospitality, freely accorded to the pilgrim; its volumes munificently presented to the foreign student; and the prayers, the blessings, the holy rites, the solemn chants, which sanctified the while both giver and receiver.

Nor can I forget either, how my own England had meanwhile become the solicitude of the same unwearied eye: how Augustine was sent to us by Gregory; how he fainted in the way at the tidings of our fierceness, and, but for the Pope, would have shrunk as from an impossible expedition; how he was forced on "in weakness and in fear and in much trembling," until he had achieved the conquest of the island to Christ. Nor, again, how it came to pass that, when Augustine died and his work slackened, another Pope, unwearied still, sent three saints from Rome, to ennoble and refine the people Augustine had converted. Three holy men set out for England together, of different nations: Theodore, an Asiatic Greek, from Tarsus; Adrian, an African; Bennett alone a Saxon, for Peter knows no distinction of races in his ecumenical work. They came with theology and science in their train; with relics, with pictures, with manuscripts of the Holy Fathers and the Greek classics; and Theodore and Adrian founded schools, secular and monastic, all over England, while Bennett brought to the north the large library he had collected in foreign parts, and, with plans and ornamental work from France, erected a church of stone, under the invocation of St. Peter, after the Roman fashion, "which,' says the historian [Note 2], "he most affected." I call to mind how St. Wilfrid, St. John of Beverley, St. Bede, and other saintly men, carried on the good work in the following generations, and how from that time forth the two islands, England and Ireland, in a dark and dreary age, were the two lights of Christendom, and had no claims on each other, and no thought of self, save in the interchange of kind offices and the rivalry of love.

O memorable time, when St. Aidan and the Irish monks went up to Lindisfarne and Melrose, and taught the Saxon youth, and when a St. Cuthbert and a St. Eata repaid their charitable toil! O blessed days of peace and confidence, when the Celtic Mailduf penetrated to Malmesbury in the south, which has inherited his name, and founded there the famous school which gave birth to the great St. Aldhelm! O precious seal and testimony of Gospel unity, when, as Aldhelm in turn tells us, the English went to Ireland "numerous as bees;" when the Saxon St. Egbert and St. Willibrod, preachers to the heathen Frisons, made the voyage to Ireland to prepare themselves for their work; and when from Ireland went forth to Germany the two noble Ewalds, Saxons also, to earn the crown of martyrdom! Such a period, indeed, so rich in grace, in peace, in love, and in good works, could only last for a season; but, even when the light was to pass away from them, the sister islands were destined, not to forfeit, but to transmit it together. The time came when the neighbouring continental country was in turn to hold the mission which they had exercised so long and well; and when to it they made over their honourable office, faithful to the alliance of two hundred years, they made it a joint act. Alcuin was the pupil both of the English and of the Irish schools; and when Charlemagne would revive science and letters in his own France, it was Alcuin, the representative both of the Saxon and the Celt, who was the chief of those who went forth to supply the need of the great Emperor. Such was the foundation of the School of Paris, from which, in the course of centuries, sprang the famous University, the glory of the middle ages.

The past never returns; the course of events, old in its texture, is ever new in its colouring and fashion. England and Ireland are not what they once were, but Rome is where it was, and St. Peter is the same: his zeal, his charity, his mission, his gifts are all the same. He of old made the two islands one by giving them joint work of teaching; and now surely he is giving us a like mission, and we shall become one again, while we zealously and lovingly fulfil it.

Notes

1. *Vide* M. L'Abbé Lalanne's recent work.

2. Cressy.

Discourse 5: Knowledge Its Own End

A UNIVERSITY may be considered with reference either to its Students or to its Studies; and the principle, that all Knowledge is a whole and the separate Sciences parts of one, which I have hitherto been using in behalf of its studies, is equally important when we direct our attention to its students. Now then I turn to the students, and shall consider the education which, by virtue of this principle, a University will give them; and thus I shall be introduced, Gentlemen, to the second question, which I proposed to discuss, viz., whether and in what sense its teaching, viewed relatively to the taught, carries the attribute of Utility along with it.

I have said that all branches of knowledge are connected together, because the subject-matter of knowledge is intimately united in itself, as being the acts and the work of the Creator. Hence it is that the Sciences, into which our knowledge may be said to be cast, have multiplied bearings one on another, and an internal sympathy, and admit, or rather demand, comparison and adjustment. They complete, correct, balance each other. This consideration, if well-founded, must be taken into account, not only as regards the attainment of truth, which is their common end, but as regards the influence which they exercise upon those whose education consists in the study of them. I have said already, that to give undue prominence to one is to be unjust to another; to neglect or supersede these is to divert those from their proper object. It is to unsettle the boundary lines between science and science, to disturb their action, to destroy the harmony which binds them together. Such a proceeding will have a corresponding effect when introduced into a place of education. There is no science but tells a different tale, when viewed as a portion of a whole, from what it is likely to suggest when taken by itself, without the safeguard, as I may call it, of others.

Let me make use of an illustration. In the combination of colours, very different effects are produced by a difference in their selection and juxtaposition; red, green, and white, change their shades, according to the contrast to which they are submitted. And, in like manner, the drift and meaning of a branch of knowledge varies with the company in which it is introduced to the student. If his reading is confined simply to one subject, however such division of labour may favour the advancement of a particular pursuit, a point into which I do not here enter, certainly it has a tendency to contract his mind. If it is incorporated with others, it depends on those others as to the kind of influence which it exerts upon him. Thus the Classics, which in England are the means of refining the taste, have in France subserved the spread of revolutionary and deistical doctrines. In Metaphysics, again, Butler's Analogy of Religion, which has had so much to do with the conversion to the Catholic faith of members of the University of Oxford, appeared to Pitt and others, who had received a different training, to operate only in the direction of infidelity. And so again, Watson, Bishop of Llandaff, as I think he tells us in the narrative of his life, felt the science of Mathematics to indispose the mind to religious belief, while others see in its investigations the best parallel, and thereby defence, of the Christian Mysteries. In like manner, I suppose, Arcesilas would not have handled logic as Aristotle, nor Aristotle have criticized poets as Plato; yet reasoning and poetry are subject to scientific rules.

It is a great point then to enlarge the range of studies which a University professes, even for the sake of the students; and, though they cannot pursue every subject which is open to them, they will be the gainers by living among those and under those who represent the whole circle. This I conceive to be the advantage of a seat of universal learning, considered as a place of education. An assemblage of learned men, zealous for their own sciences, and rivals of each other, are brought, by familiar intercourse and for the sake of intellectual peace, to adjust together the claims and relations of their respective subjects of investigation. They learn to respect, to consult, to aid each other. Thus is created a pure and clear atmosphere of thought, which the student also breathes, though in his own case he only pursues a few sciences out of the multitude. He profits by an intellectual tradition, which is independent of particular teachers, which guides him in his choice of subjects, and duly interprets for him those which he chooses. He apprehends the great outlines of knowledge, the principles on which it rests, the scale of its parts, its lights and its shades, its great points and its little, as he otherwise cannot apprehend them. Hence it is that his education is called "Liberal." A habit of mind is formed which lasts through life, of which the attributes are, freedom, equitableness, calmness, moderation, and wisdom; or what in a former

Discourse I have ventured to call a philosophical habit. This then I would assign as the special fruit of the education furnished at a University, as contrasted with other places of teaching or modes of teaching. This is the main purpose of a University in its treatment of its students.

And now the question is asked me, What is the *use* of it? and my answer will constitute the main subject of the Discourses which are to follow.

Cautious and practical thinkers, I say, will ask of me, what, after all, is the gain of this Philosophy, of which I make such account, and from which I promise so much. Even supposing it to enable us to exercise the degree of trust exactly due to every science respectively, and to estimate precisely the value of every truth which is anywhere to be found, how are we better for this master view of things, which I have been extolling? Does it not reverse the principle of the division of labour? will practical objects be obtained better or worse by its cultivation? to what then does it lead? where does it end? what does it do? how does it profit? what does it promise? Particular sciences are respectively the basis of definite arts, which carry on to results tangible and beneficial the truths which are the subjects of the knowledge attained; what is the Art of this science of sciences? what is the fruit of such a Philosophy? what are we proposing to effect, what inducements do we hold out to the Catholic community, when we set about the enterprise of founding a University?

I am asked what is the end of University Education, and of the Liberal or Philosophical Knowledge which I conceive it to impart: I answer, that what I have already said has been sufficient to show that it has a very tangible, real, and sufficient end, though the end cannot be divided from that knowledge itself. Knowledge is capable of being its own end. Such is the constitution of the human mind, that any kind of knowledge, if it be really such, is its own reward. And if this is true of all knowledge, it is true also of that special Philosophy, which I have made to consist in a comprehensive view of truth in all its branches, of the relations of science to science, of their mutual bearings, and their respective values. What the worth of such an acquirement is, compared with other objects which we seek,—wealth or power or honour or the conveniences and comforts of life, I do not profess here to discuss; but I would maintain, and mean to show, that it is an object, in its own nature so really and undeniably good, as to be the compensation of a great deal of thought in the compassing, and a great deal of trouble in the attaining.

Now, when I say that Knowledge is, not merely a means to something beyond it, or the preliminary of certain arts into which it naturally resolves, but an end sufficient to rest in and to pursue for its own sake, surely I am uttering no paradox, for I am stating what is both intelligible in itself, and has ever been the common judgment of philosophers and the ordinary feeling of mankind. I am saying what at least the public opinion of this day ought to be slow to deny, considering how much we have heard of late years, in opposition to Religion, of entertaining, curious, and various knowledge. I am but saying what whole volumes have been written to illustrate, viz., by a "selection from the records of Philosophy, Literature, and Art, in all ages and countries, of a body of examples, to show how the most unpropitious circumstances have been unable to conquer an ardent desire for the acquisition of knowledge." [Note 1] That further advantages accrue to us and redound to others by its possession, over and above what it is in itself, I am very far indeed from denying; but, independent of these, we are satisfying a direct need of our nature in its very acquisition; and, whereas our nature, unlike that of the inferior creation, does not at once reach its perfection, but depends, in order to it, on a number of external aids and appliances, Knowledge, as one of the principal of these, is valuable for what its very presence in us does for us after the manner of a habit, even though it be turned to no further account, nor subserve any direct end.

Hence it is that Cicero, in enumerating the various heads of mental excellence, lays down the pursuit of Knowledge for its own sake, as the first of them. "This pertains most of all to human nature," he says, "for we are all of us drawn to the pursuit of Knowledge; in which to excel we consider excellent, whereas to mistake, to err, to be ignorant, to be deceived, is both an evil and a disgrace." [Note 2] And he considers Knowledge the very first object to which we are attracted, after the supply of our physical wants. After the calls and duties of our animal existence, as they may be termed, as regards ourselves, our family, and our neighbours, follows, he tells us, "the search after truth. Accordingly, as soon as we escape from the pressure of necessary cares, forthwith we desire to see, to hear, and to learn; and consider the knowledge of what is hidden or is wonderful a condition of our happiness."

This passage, though it is but one of many similar passages in a multitude of authors, I take for the very reason that it is so familiarly known to us; and I wish you to observe, Gentlemen, how distinctly it separates the pursuit of Knowledge from those ulterior objects to which certainly it can be made to conduce, and which are, I suppose, solely contemplated by the persons who would ask of me the use of a University or Liberal Education. So far from dreaming of the cultivation of Knowledge directly and mainly in order to our physical comfort and enjoyment, for the sake of life and person, of health, of the conjugal and family union, of the social tie and civil security, the great Orator implies, that it is only after our physical and political needs are supplied, and when we are "free from necessary duties and cares," that we are in a condition for "desiring to see, to hear, and to learn." Nor does he contemplate in the least degree the reflex or subsequent action of Knowledge, when acquired, upon those material goods which we set out by securing before we seek it; on the contrary, he expressly denies its bearing upon social life altogether, strange as such a procedure is to those who live after the rise of the Baconian philosophy, and he cautions us against such a cultivation of it as will interfere with our duties to our fellow-creatures. "All these methods," he says, "are engaged in the investigation of truth; by the pursuit of which to be carried off from public occupations is a transgression of duty. For the praise of virtue lies altogether in action; yet intermissions often occur, and then we recur to such pursuits; not to say that the incessant activity of the mind is vigorous enough to carry us on in the pursuit of knowledge, even without any exertion of our own." The idea of benefiting society by means of "the pursuit of science and knowledge" did not enter at all into the motives which he would assign for their cultivation.

This was the ground of the opposition which the elder Cato made to the introduction of Greek Philosophy among his countrymen, when Carneades and his companions, on occasion of their embassy, were charming the Roman youth with their eloquent expositions of it. The fit representative of a practical people, Cato estimated every thing by what it produced; whereas the Pursuit of Knowledge promised nothing beyond Knowledge itself. He despised that refinement or enlargement of mind of which he had no experience.

Things, which can bear to be cut off from every thing else and yet persist in living, must have life in themselves; pursuits, which issue in nothing, and still maintain their ground for ages, which are regarded as admirable, though they have not as yet proved themselves to be useful, must have their sufficient end in themselves, whatever it turn out to be. And we are brought to the same conclusion by considering the force of the epithet, by which the knowledge under consideration is popularly designated. It is common to speak of "*liberal* knowledge," of the "*liberal* arts and studies," and of a "*liberal* education," as the especial characteristic or property of a University and of a gentleman; what is really meant by the word? Now, first, in its grammatical sense it is opposed to *servile*; and by "servile work" is understood, as our catechisms inform us, bodily labour, mechanical employment, and the like, in which the mind has little or no part. Parallel to such servile works are those arts, if they deserve the name, of which the poet speaks [Note 3], which owe their origin and their method to hazard, not to skill; as, for instance, the practice and operations of an empiric. As far as this contrast may be considered as a guide into the meaning of the word, liberal education and liberal pursuits are exercises of mind, of reason, of reflection.

But we want something more for its explanation, for there are bodily exercises which are liberal, and mental exercises which are not so. For instance, in ancient times the practitioners in medicine were commonly slaves; yet it was an art as intellectual in its nature, in spite of the pretence, fraud, and quackery with which it might then, as now, be debased, as it was heavenly in its aim. And so in like manner, we contrast a liberal education with a commercial education or a professional; yet no one can deny that commerce and the professions afford scope for the highest and most diversified powers of mind. There is then a great variety of intellectual exercises, which are not technically called "liberal;" on the other hand, I say, there are exercises of the body which do receive that appellation. Such, for instance, was the palæstra, in ancient times; such the Olympic games, in which strength and dexterity of body as well as of mind gained the prize. In Xenophon we read of the young Persian nobility being taught to ride on horseback and to speak the truth; both being among the accomplishments of a gentleman. War, too, however rough a profession, has ever been accounted liberal, unless in cases when it becomes heroic, which would introduce us to another subject.

Now comparing these instances together, we shall have no difficulty in determining the principle of this apparent variation in the application of the term which I am examining. Manly games, or games of skill, or military prowess, though bodily, are, it seems, accounted liberal; on the other hand, what is merely professional, though highly intellectual, nay, though liberal in comparison of trade and manual labour, is not simply called liberal, and mercantile occupations are not liberal at all. Why this distinction? because that alone is liberal knowledge, which stands on its own pretensions, which is independent of sequel, expects no complement, refuses to be *informed* (as it is called) by any end, or absorbed into any art, in order duly to present itself to our contemplation. The most ordinary pursuits have this specific character, if they are self-sufficient and complete; the highest lose it, when they minister to something beyond them. It is absurd to balance, in point of worth and importance, a treatise on reducing fractures with a game of cricket or a fox-chase; yet of the two the bodily exercise has that quality which we call "liberal," and the intellectual has it not. And so of the learned professions altogether, considered merely as professions; although one of them be the most popularly beneficial, and another the most politically important, and the third the most intimately divine of all human pursuits, yet the very greatness of their end, the health of the body, or of the commonwealth, or of the soul, diminishes, not increases, their claim to the appellation "liberal," and that still more, if they are cut down to the strict exigencies of that end. If, for instance, Theology, instead of being cultivated as a contemplation, be limited to the purposes of the pulpit or be represented by the catechism, it loses,—not its usefulness, not its divine character, not its meritoriousness (rather it gains a claim upon these titles by such charitable condescension),—but it does lose the particular attribute which I am illustrating; just as a face worn by tears and fasting loses its beauty, or a labourer's hand loses its delicateness;—for Theology thus exercised is not simple knowledge, but rather is an art or a business making use of Theology. And thus it appears that even what is supernatural need not be liberal, nor need a hero be a gentleman, for the plain reason that one idea is not another idea. And in like manner the Baconian Philosophy, by using its physical sciences in the service of man, does thereby transfer them from the order of Liberal Pursuits to, I do not say the inferior, but the distinct class of the Useful. And, to take a different instance, hence again, as is evident, whenever personal gain is the motive, still more distinctive an effect has it upon the character of a given pursuit; thus racing, which was a liberal exercise in Greece, forfeits its rank in times like these, so far as it is made the occasion of gambling.

All that I have been now saying is summed up in a few characteristic words of the great Philosopher. "Of possessions," he says, "those rather are useful, which bear fruit; those *liberal, which tend to enjoyment.* By fruitful, I mean, which yield revenue; by enjoyable, where *nothing accrues of consequence beyond the using.*" [Note 4]

Do not suppose, that in thus appealing to the ancients, I am throwing back the world two thousand years, and fettering Philosophy with the reasonings of paganism. While the world lasts, will Aristotle's doctrine on these matters last, for he is the oracle of nature and of truth. While we are men, we cannot help, to a great extent, being Aristotelians, for the great Master does but analyze the thoughts, feelings, views, and opinions of human kind. He has told us the meaning of our own words and ideas, before we were born. In many subject-matters, to think correctly, is to think like Aristotle; and we are his disciples whether we will or no, though we may not know it. Now, as to the particular instance before us, the word "liberal" as applied to Knowledge and Education, expresses a specific idea, which ever has been, and ever will be, while the nature of man is the same, just as the idea of the Beautiful is specific, or of the Sublime, or of the

Ridiculous, or of the Sordid. It is in the world now, it was in the world then; and, as in the case of the dogmas of faith, it is illustrated by a continuous historical tradition, and never was out of the world, from the time it came into it. There have indeed been differences of opinion from time to time, as to what pursuits and what arts came under that idea, but such differences are but an additional evidence of its reality. That idea must have a substance in it, which has maintained its ground amid these conflicts and changes, which has ever served as a standard to measure things withal, which has passed from mind to mind unchanged, when there was so much to colour, so much to influence any notion or thought whatever, which was not founded in our very nature. Were it a mere generalization, it would have varied with the subjects from which it was generalized; but though its subjects vary with the age, it varies not itself. The palæstra may seem a liberal exercise to Lycurgus, and illiberal to Seneca; coach-driving and prize-fighting may be recognized in Elis, and be condemned in England; music may be despicable in the eyes of certain moderns, and be in the highest place with Aristotle and Plato,—(and the case is the same in the particular application of the idea of Beauty, or of Goodness, or of Moral Virtue, there is a difference of tastes, a difference of judgments)—still these variations imply, instead of discrediting, the archetypal idea, which is but a previous hypothesis or condition, by means of which issue is joined between contending opinions, and without which there would be nothing to dispute about.

I consider, then, that I am chargeable with no paradox, when I speak of a Knowledge which is its own end, when I call it liberal knowledge, or a gentleman's knowledge, when I educate for it, and make it the scope of a University. And still less am I incurring such a charge, when I make this acquisition consist, not in Knowledge in a vague and ordinary sense, but in that Knowledge which I have especially called Philosophy or, in an extended sense of the word, Science;

for whatever claims Knowledge has to be considered as a good, these it has in a higher degree when it is viewed not vaguely, not popularly, but precisely and transcendently as Philosophy. Knowledge, I say, is then especially liberal, or sufficient for itself, apart from every external and ulterior object, when and so far as it is philosophical, and this I proceed to show.

Now bear with me, Gentlemen, if what I am about to say, has at first sight a fanciful appearance. Philosophy, then, or Science, is related to Knowledge in this way:—Knowledge is called by the name of Science or Philosophy, when it is acted upon, informed, or if I may use a strong figure, impregnated by Reason. Reason is the principle of that intrinsic fecundity of Knowledge, which, to those who possess it, is its especial value, and which dispenses with the necessity of their looking abroad for any end to rest upon external to itself. Knowledge, indeed, when thus exalted into a scientific form, is also power; not only is it excellent in itself, but whatever such excellence may be, it is something more, it has a result beyond itself. Doubtless; but that is a further consideration, with which I am not concerned. I only say that, prior to its being a power, it is a good; that it is, not only an instrument, but an end. I know well it may resolve itself into an art, and terminate in a mechanical process, and in tangible fruit; but it also may fall back upon that Reason which informs it, and resolve itself into Philosophy. In one case it is called Useful Knowledge, in the other Liberal. The same person may cultivate it in both ways at once; but this again is a matter foreign to my subject; here I do but say that there are two ways of using Knowledge, and in matter of fact those who use it in one way are not likely to use it in the other, or at least in a very limited measure. You see, then, here are two methods of Education; the end of the one is to be philosophical, of the other to be mechanical; the one rises towards general ideas, the other is exhausted upon what is particular and external. Let me not be thought to deny the necessity, or to decry the benefit, of such attention to what is particular and practical, as belongs to the useful or mechanical arts; life could not go on without them; we owe our daily welfare to them; their exercise is the duty of the many, and we owe to the many a debt of gratitude for fulfilling that duty. I only say that Knowledge, in proportion as it tends more and more to be particular, ceases to be Knowledge. It is a question whether Knowledge can in any proper sense be predicated of the brute creation; without pretending to metaphysical exactness of phraseology, which would be unsuitable to an occasion like this, I say, it seems to me improper to call that passive sensation, or perception of things, which brutes seem to possess, by the name of Knowledge. When I speak of Knowledge, I mean something intellectual, something which grasps what it perceives through the senses; something which takes a view of things; which sees more than the senses convey; which reasons upon what it sees, and while it sees; which invests it with an idea. It expresses itself, not in a mere enunciation, but by an enthymeme: it is of the nature of science from the first, and in this consists its dignity. The principle of real dignity in Knowledge, its worth, its desirableness, considered irrespectively of its results, is this germ within it of a scientific or a philosophical process. This is how it comes to be an end in itself; this is why it admits of being called Liberal. Not to know the relative disposition of things is the state of slaves or children; to have mapped out the Universe is the boast, or at least the ambition, of Philosophy.

Moreover, such knowledge is not a mere extrinsic or accidental advantage, which is ours today and another's tomorrow, which may be got up from a book, and easily forgotten again, which we can command or communicate at our pleasure, which we can borrow for the occasion, carry about in our hand, and take into the market; it is an acquired illumination, it is a habit, a personal possession, and an inward endowment. And this is the reason, why it is more correct, as well as more usual, to speak of a University as a place of education, than of instruction, though, when knowledge is concerned, instruction would at first sight have seemed the more appropriate word. We are instructed, for instance, in manual exercises, in the fine and useful arts, in trades, and in ways of business; for these are methods, which have little or no effect upon the mind itself, are contained in rules committed to memory, to tradition, or to use, and bear upon an end external to themselves. But education is a higher word; it implies an action upon our mental nature, and the formation of a character; it is something individual and permanent, and is commonly spoken of in connexion with religion and virtue. When, then, we speak of the communication of Knowledge as being Education, we thereby really imply that that Knowledge is a state or condition of mind; and since cultivation of mind is surely worth seeking for its own sake, we are thus brought once more to the conclusion, which the word "Liberal" and the word "Philosophy" have already suggested, that there is a Knowledge, which is desirable, though nothing come of it, as being of itself a treasure, and a sufficient remuneration of years of labour.

This, then, is the answer which I am prepared to give to the question with which I opened this Discourse. Before going on to speak of the object of the Church in taking up Philosophy, and the uses to which she puts it, I am prepared to maintain that Philosophy is its own end, and, as I conceive, I have now begun the proof of it. I am prepared to maintain that there is a knowledge worth possessing for what it is, and not merely for what it does; and what minutes remain to me today I shall devote to the removal of some portion of the indistinctness and confusion with which the subject may in some minds be surrounded.

It may be objected then, that, when we profess to seek Knowledge for some end or other beyond itself, whatever it be, we speak intelligibly; but that, whatever men may have said, however obstinately the idea may have kept its ground from age to age, still it is simply unmeaning to say that we seek Knowledge for its own sake, and for nothing else; for that it ever leads to something beyond itself, which therefore is its end, and the cause why it is desirable;—moreover, that this end is twofold, either of this world or of the next; that all knowledge is cultivated either for secular objects or for eternal; that if it is directed to secular objects, it is called Useful Knowledge, if to eternal, Religious or Christian Knowledge;—in consequence, that if, as I have allowed, this Liberal Knowledge does not benefit the body or estate, it ought to benefit the soul; but if the fact be really so, that it is neither a physical nor a secular good on the one hand, nor a moral good on the other, it cannot be a good at all, and is not worth the trouble which is necessary for its acquisition.

And then I may be reminded that the professors of this Liberal or Philosophical Knowledge have themselves, in every age, recognized this exposition of the matter, and have submitted to the issue in which it terminates; for they have ever been attempting to make men virtuous; or, if not, at least have assumed that refinement of mind was virtue, and that they themselves were the virtuous portion of mankind. This they have professed on the one hand; and on the other, they have utterly failed in their professions, so as ever to make themselves a proverb among men, and a laughing-stock both to the grave and the dissipated portion of mankind, in consequence of them. Thus they have furnished against themselves both the ground and the means of their own exposure, without any trouble at all to any one else. In a word, from the time that Athens was the University of the world, what has Philosophy taught men, but to promise without practising, and to aspire without attaining? What has the deep and lofty thought of its disciples ended in but eloquent words? Nay, what has its teaching ever meditated, when it was boldest in its remedies for human ill, beyond charming us to sleep by its lessons, that we might feel nothing at all? like some melodious air, or rather like those strong and transporting perfumes, which at first spread their sweetness over every thing they touch, but in a little while do but offend in proportion as they once pleased us. Did Philosophy support Cicero under the disfavour of the fickle populace, or nerve Seneca to oppose an imperial tyrant? It abandoned Brutus, as he sorrowfully confessed, in his greatest need, and it forced Cato, as his panegyrist strangely boasts, into the false position of defying heaven. How few can be counted among its professors, who, like Polemo, were thereby converted from a profligate course, or like Anaxagoras, thought the world well lost in exchange for its possession? The philosopher in Rasselas taught a superhuman doctrine, and then succumbed without an effort to a trial of human affection.

"He discoursed," we are told, "with great energy on the government of the passions. His look was venerable, his action graceful, his pronunciation clear, and his diction elegant. He showed, with great strength of sentiment and variety of illustration, that human nature is degraded and debased, when the lower faculties predominate over the higher. He communicated the various precepts given, from time to time, for the conquest of passion, and displayed the happiness of those who had obtained the important victory, after which man is no longer the slave of fear, nor the fool of hope. ... He enumerated many examples of heroes immoveable by pain or pleasure, who looked with indifference on those modes or accidents to which the vulgar give the names of good and evil."

Rasselas in a few days found the philosopher in a room half darkened, with his eyes misty, and his face pale. "Sir," said he, "you have come at a time when all human friendship is useless; what I suffer cannot be remedied, what I have lost cannot be supplied. My daughter, my only daughter, from whose tenderness I expected all the comforts of my age, died last night of a fever." "Sir," said the prince, "mortality is an event by which a wise man can never be surprised; we know that death is always near, and it should therefore always be expected." "Young man," answered the philosopher, "you speak like one who has never felt the pangs of separation." "Have you, then, forgot the precept," said Rasselas, "which you so powerfully enforced? . . . consider that external things are naturally variable, but truth and reason are always the same." "What comfort," said the mourner, "can truth and reason afford me? Of what effect are they now, but to tell me that my daughter will not be restored?"

Better, far better, to make no professions, you will say, than to cheat others with what we are not, and to scandalize them with what we are. The sensualist, or the man of the world, at any rate is not the victim of fine words, but pursues a reality and gains it. The Philosophy of Utility, you will say, Gentlemen, has at least done its work; and I grant it,—it aimed low, but it has fulfilled its aim. If that man of great intellect who has been its Prophet in the conduct of life played false to his own professions, he was not bound by his philosophy to be true to his friend or faithful in his trust. Moral virtue was not the line in which he undertook to instruct men; and though, as the poet calls him, he were the "meanest" of mankind, he was so in what may be called his private capacity and without any prejudice to the theory of induction. He had a right to be so, if he chose, for any thing that the Idols of the den or the theatre had to say to the contrary. His mission was the increase of physical enjoyment and social comfort [Note 5]; and most wonderfully, most awfully has he fulfilled his conception and his design. Almost day by day have we fresh and fresh shoots, and buds, and blossoms, which are to ripen into fruit, on that magical tree of Knowledge which he planted, and to which none of us perhaps, except the very poor, but owes, if not his present life, at least his daily food, his health, and general well-being. He was the divinely provided minister of temporal benefits to all of us so great, that, whatever I am forced to think of him as a man, I have not the heart, from mere gratitude, to speak of him severely. And, in spite of the tendencies of his philosophy, which are, as we see at this day, to depreciate, or to trample on Theology, he has himself, in his writings, gone out of his way, as if with a prophetic misgiving of those tendencies, to insist on it as the instrument of that beneficent Father [Note 6], who, when He came on earth in visible form, took on Him first and most prominently the office of assuaging the bodily wounds of human nature. And truly, like the old mediciner in the tale, "he sat diligently at his work, and hummed, with cheerful countenance, a pious song;" and then in turn "went out singing into the meadows so gaily, that those who had seen him from afar might well have thought it was a youth gathering flowers for his beloved, instead of an old physician gathering healing herbs in the morning dew." [Note 7]

Alas, that men, in the action of life or in their heart of hearts, are not what they seem to be in their moments of excitement, or in their trances or intoxications of genius,—so good, so noble, so serene! Alas, that Bacon too in his own way should after all be but the fellow of those heathen philosophers who in their disadvantages had some excuse for their inconsistency, and who surprise us rather in what they did say than in what they did not do! Alas, that he too, like Socrates or Seneca, must be stripped of his holy-day coat, which looks so fair, and should be but a mockery amid his most majestic gravity of phrase; and, for all his vast abilities, should, in the littleness of his own moral being, but typify the intellectual narrowness of his school! However, granting all this, heroism after all was not his philosophy:—I cannot deny he has abundantly achieved what he proposed. His is simply a Method whereby bodily discomforts and temporal wants are to be most effectually removed from the greatest number; and already, before it has shown any signs of exhaustion, the gifts of nature, in their most artificial shapes and luxurious profusion and diversity, from all quarters of the earth, are, it is undeniable, by its means brought even to our doors, and we rejoice in them.

Useful Knowledge then, I grant, has done its work; and Liberal Knowledge as certainly has not done its work,—that is, supposing, as the objectors assume, its direct end, like Religious Knowledge, is to make men better; but this I will not for an instant allow, and, unless I allow it, those objectors have said nothing to the purpose. I admit, rather I maintain, what they have been urging, for I consider Knowledge to have its end in itself. For all its friends, or its enemies, may say, I insist upon it, that it is as real a mistake to burden it with virtue or religion as with the mechanical arts. Its direct business is not to steel the soul against temptation or to console it in affliction, any more than to set the loom in motion, or to direct the steam carriage; be it ever so much the means or the condition of both material and moral advancement, still, taken by and in itself, it as little mends our hearts as it improves our temporal circumstances. And if its eulogists claim for it such a power, they commit the very same kind of encroachment on a province not their own as the political economist who should maintain that his science educated him for casuistry or diplomacy. Knowledge is one thing, virtue is another; good sense is not conscience, refinement is not humility, nor is largeness and justness of view faith. Philosophy, however enlightened, however profound, gives no command over the passions, no influential motives, no vivifying principles. Liberal Education makes not the Christian, not the Catholic, but the gentleman. It is well to be a gentlemen, it is well to have a cultivated intellect, a delicate taste, a candid, equitable, dispassionate mind, a noble and courteous bearing in the conduct of life;—these are the connatural qualities of a large knowledge; they are the objects of a University; I am advocating, I shall illustrate and insist upon them; but still, I repeat, they are no guarantee for sanctity or even for conscientiousness, they may attach to the man of the world, to the profligate, to the heartless,—pleasant, alas, and attractive as he shows when decked out in them. Taken by themselves, they do but seem to be what they are not; they look like virtue at a distance, but they are detected by close observers, and on the long run; and hence it is that they are popularly accused of pretence and hypocrisy, not, I repeat, from their own fault, but because their professors and their admirers persist in taking them for what they are not, and are officious in arrogating for them a praise to which they have no claim. Quarry the granite rock with razors, or moor the vessel with a thread of silk; then may you hope with such keen and delicate instruments as human knowledge and human reason to contend against those giants, the passion and the pride of man.

Surely we are not driven to theories of this kind, in order to vindicate the value and dignity of Liberal Knowledge. Surely the real grounds on which its pretensions rest are not so very subtle or abstruse, so very strange or improbable. Surely it is very intelligible to say, and that is what I say here, that Liberal Education, viewed in itself, is simply the cultivation of the intellect, as such, and its object is nothing more or less than intellectual excellence. Every thing has its own perfection, be it higher or lower in the scale of things; and the perfection of one is not the perfection of another. Things animate, inanimate, visible, invisible, all are good in their kind, and have a *best* of themselves, which is an object of pursuit. Why do you take such pains with your garden or your park? You see to your walks and turf and shrubberies; to your trees and drives; not as if you meant to make an orchard of the one, or corn or pasture land of the other, but because there is a special beauty in all that is goodly in wood, water, plain, and slope, brought all together by art into one shape, and grouped into one whole. Your cities are beautiful, your palaces, your public buildings, your territorial mansions, your churches; and their beauty leads to nothing beyond itself. There is a physical beauty and a moral: there is a beauty of person, there is a beauty of our moral being, which is natural virtue; and in like manner there is a beauty, there is a perfection, of the intellect. There is an ideal perfection in these various subject-matters, towards which individual instances are seen to rise, and which are the standards for all instances whatever. The Greek divinities and demigods, as the statuary has moulded them, with their symmetry of figure, and their high forehead and their regular features, are the perfection of physical beauty. The heroes, of whom history tells, Alexander, or Cæsar, or Scipio, or Saladin, are the representatives of that magnanimity or self-mastery which is the greatness of human nature. Christianity too has its heroes, and in the supernatural order, and we call them Saints. The artist puts before him beauty of feature and form; the poet, beauty of mind; the preacher, the beauty of grace: then intellect too, I repeat, has its beauty, and it has those who aim at it. To open the mind, to correct it, to refine it, to enable it to know, and to digest, master, rule, and use its knowledge, to give it power over its own faculties, application, flexibility, method, critical exactness, sagacity, resource, address, eloquent expression, is an object as intelligible (for here we are inquiring, not what the object of a Liberal Education is worth, nor what use the Church makes of it, but what it is in itself), I say, an object as intelligible as the cultivation of virtue, while, at the same time, it is absolutely distinct from it.

This indeed is but a temporal object, and a transitory possession; but so are other things in themselves which we make much of and pursue. The moralist will tell us that man, in all his functions, is but a flower which blossoms and fades, except so far as a higher principle breathes upon him, and makes him and what he is immortal. Body and mind are carried on into an eternal state of being by the gifts of Divine Munificence; but at first they do but fail in a failing world; and if the powers of intellect decay, the powers of the body have decayed

before them, and, as an Hospital or an Almshouse, though its end be
ephemeral, may be sanctified to the service of religion, so surely may
a University, even were it nothing more than I have as yet described
it. We attain to heaven by using this world well, though it is to pass
away; we perfect our nature, not by undoing it, but by adding to it
what is more than nature, and directing it towards aims higher than
its own.

Notes

1. Pursuit of Knowledge under Difficulties. Introd.

2. Cicer. Offic. init.

3. [*Techne tuchen esterxe kai tuche technen.*] Vid. Arist. Nic. Ethic. vi.

4. Aristot. Rhet. i. 5.

5. It will be seen that on the whole I agree with Lord Macaulay in his
   Essay on Bacon's Philosophy. I do not know whether he would agree
   with me.

6. De Augment. iv. 2, vid. Macaulay's Essay; vid. also "In principio
   operis ad Deum Patrem, Deum Verbum, Deum Spiritum, preces
   fundimus humillimas et ardentissimas, ut humani generis
   ærumnarum memores, et peregrinationis istius vitæ, in quâ dies
   paucos et malos terimus, *novis suis eleemosynis, per manus nostras,*
   familiam humanam dotare dignentur. Atque illud insuper supplices
   rogamus, ne *humana divinis officiant*; neve *ex reseratione viarum
   sensûs*, et accensione majore luminis naturalis, *aliquid incredulitatis*
   et noctis, animis nostris erga divina mysteria oriatur," etc. *Præf.*
   Instaur. Magn.

7. Fouque's Unknown Patient.

ACKNOWLEDGMENTS

We would like to especially thank the following people for their indispensable help in the creation of this book: Harry Crocker, Lauren Snyder, Regnery Publishing, Michael Knowles, Stephanie Gordon, Addison Smith, Campus Reform, Quillette, Claire Lehmann, Will Knowland, and Peter Boghossian.

How I Left Academia, or, How Academia Left Me

When I first encountered the discipline of philosophy as an undergraduate at West Point some twenty years ago, I was put into a state of awe. Encountering the ideas of Plato and Aristotle, Kant and Hume, and Berkeley and Russell for the very first time felt like I was being let in on some ancient and esoteric form of knowledge, some sort of secret language invisible to the uninitiated. Leaving the classroom each day, debating and conversing with other students over these new and earth-shattering concepts and questions felt like a kind of drug trip, like I was Neo being shown the code for the Matrix. For those years and for who I was at the time, it was truly a mind-altering and life-changing experience. And while the questions shook my sense of certainty to the core, filling my head with all sorts of doubts, I nonetheless remained certain of one thing: that Socrates was ultimately right and that the unexamined life was indeed not worth living.

I was compelled so much so by these philosophical questions and ideas that I would later be moved to terminate what was, at the time, a fruitful career as a U.S. Army officer, to turn down several lucrative white-collar jobs thereafter, and to shove all my chips into the center of the playing table in hopes of one day becoming a professional analytic philosopher. Now, after a decade of being within the ivory tower, a decade of seeing how the sausage is made and witnessing firsthand the business that academia really is, I've determined, quite sadly, that the discipline of academic philosophy—and the university system more generally—has become little more than an indoctrination center for woke leftist ideology and the antithesis of its original aim and purpose. That being said, this essay is my explanation of how and why I'm leaving academia, or, more appropriately, how academia ended up leaving me.

My cynicism towards academia was not always this way, however. Coming away jaded from the Bush administration's handling of the Iraq War in my mid-twenties, believing that we as American citizens had some basic duties to look out for animals, the environment, and for the poor, and thinking that African Americans still had some reasonable and justified grievances because of slavery, I found myself entering into graduate school at the beginning of the Obama years as a self-described "center-left" liberal.

The beginning few years of my time in grad school were a combination of exhilaration, possibility, and most of all, vindication. Unlike my time in the stifling, hyper-conformist atmosphere of the military, now I was finally home, around *my* people—people who were thoughtful, open-minded, knowledgeable, worldly, lovers of ideas, and appreciators of the life of mind. No longer the odd-duck soldier who thought too much, I felt, for the very first time in my adult life, like I was finally accepted.

For the most part, many of my professors and my graduate peers found me to be something of a refreshing anomaly. I was the thoughtful, philosophical soldier, critical of our country's recent wars. During that time period, I could also sleep easily at night with a clear conscience knowing I was now one of "the good people" on the Left, a proud "bleeding heart," no longer immersed among the religious nut-jobs, the money-obsessed corporate shills, the war-hawks, and the racists who comprised the ranks of the Right. I was none of these things. Rather, I was the open-minded, compassionate, slightly left-leaning, "nuanced centrist," who could just as easily have a chat with the frontline infantryman from Nebraska as I could with the ivory-tower academic from Oxford while serving as a kind of bridge between these two worlds, synthesizing a dialogue between left and right, mind and body, theory and practice. At least this was the story that I told myself.

In retrospect, the cracks in the liberal dam were always there from the very beginning, but I was either too distracted, too busy, too intimidated, too career obsessed, or just too willfully ignorant to truly see the cracks, let alone acknowledge them or their ultimate ideological direction of travel. At first, such fissures were easy to dismiss or hand-wave away. Certainly, the more fringe versions of the Left, what Richard Rorty referred to as the "cultural left," I could openly critique with the tolerance or even support of my professors or graduate peers. "We do *analytic* philosophy here, arguments from arm-chair first principles," I was re-assured, "not that postmodern nonsense you find on the edges of some anthropology or lit crit department. That's the *far* left. We're on the *moderate, sensible* left. Have you ever read Rawls?"

For a certain moment in time, I could arguably get on board with such thinking. What barbarian didn't believe that we had some duty to animals and to the environment? To future generations? To fellow citizens who were most vulnerable? To soldiers and civilians alike?

Somewhere around the spring of 2017, however, amidst the cultural backlash against Trumpism, coupled with the mainstream explosion of transgenderism, intersectionality, critical race theory, and mass campus protests against perceived "far-right extremist" speakers, the academy I once knew and loved seemed to go completely off the rails. The mask of the "tolerant," "open-minded" left suddenly fell off and, for the very first time, I came to realize that the ivory tower and so-called "free market of ideas" was not above and beyond or as immune to the present social zeitgeist as I once had thought.

With few exceptions, present-day analytic philosophy and academia more generally exhibit hardly *any* of the values and virtues that they explicitly profess to care so much about: tolerance, open-mindedness, regard for different perspectives, epistemic charity, a willingness to entertain pluralistic viewpoints, rational and dispassionate assessment of arguments, lack of ad hoc justifications, lack of ad hominem attacks, operating from arm-chair first principles, and a willingness to follow the entailments of premises to their logical conclusions come hell or high water. Nearly all of these epistemic virtues are markedly and demonstrably absent in present-day academia and present-day academics save for a Hillsdale or a Claremont, a Jordan Peterson or a Peter Boghossian, a James Lindsay or a Thomas Sowell.

Rather, academics on the Left now make their arguments primarily by means of social pressure and stigmatization, intimidation, group-struggle sessions, virtue signaling, and online reputational assassination in the form of labeling their opponents as "extremists," "racists," "phobes," "bigots," or worse, rather than engaging with their opponents' arguments on their own merits. More perplexing still, such folks often do so having fully convinced themselves that they are somehow oppressed victims and scrappy underdogs "speaking truth to power" against impossible odds as part of some revolutionary underground resistance movement while garnering support from nearly *every* major Western institution imaginable from Hollywood to Big Business, and from the Queen of England to OREO cookies.

Mark Bray, for instance, author of *Antifa:* The *Antifascist Handbook*, nearly openly calls for overt violence against anyone who disagrees with his group's political vision while promoting his work on Amazon's bestseller list and enjoying the safety of a professorship at Rutgers. Feminist journalist, Laurie Penny, promotes her "radical" viewpoints, too disruptive and controversial for everyday consumption, at the "Festival of Dangerous Ideas" officially sponsored by the Sydney Opera House and the city of Sydney. And LGBTQ+ philosopher Rebecca Kukla is able to tell her opponents on Twitter to "suck her queer cock" while maintaining a comfortable tenure as Senior Research Scholar of Ethics at (nominally Catholic) Georgetown while suffering zero professional backlash. Meanwhile veteran suicide rates in this country get shoved behind a superficial veil of "Thank you for your service," but please someone stop the presses because "trans people are dying," whatever the hell that even means. Still *these* folks are somehow "the marginalized."

If not actively taking part in ceaseless woke attacks as part of the small but highly vocal far-left vanguard, the majority of academics (I'd wager even a *super-majority* of academics) have now been completely cowed into silence and complicity by the intersectional ideologues, burying their heads deeper in the sand, promising themselves that on some far-off future day—once the professional and social climate somehow improves, *once someone else* has stuck his neck out and cleared a safer path, once they achieve tenure, department head, emeritus status, enough grant money, et cetera—*then* the gloves will suddenly come off, *then* they will magically turn into fire-breathing lions, *then* they will finally speak their minds.

If human psychology and human history are any guide, then the trend suggests that such a day will never come for such persons, since feeding that muscle of complicity and inaction only serves to strengthen it, and "tenure" will most likely become swapped out with some new placeholder-excuse to put off standing up and speaking the truth for just one more day. Maybe the cannibalization will somehow miss them if they just stay silent, just bend the knee, and just disavow long enough. The writings of Hannah Arendt, Martin Niemöller, and Aleksandr Solzhenitsyn, to name just a few, suggest the supreme folly and ultimate end-state of such a strategy of never-ending appeasement. This, however, is the new normal within the "free market of ideas."

Stay within the safe lanes of extremely clever, overly technical, and ultimately *inconsequential* intellectual discourse, and you will likely be able to make tenure and have a long and prosperous academic career. Say something the least bit critical of the current intersectional orthodoxy or, conversely, say something the least bit positive about Christianity, men, the free market, liberty, merit, America, or the values of Western civilization, and you are instantly relegated to *persona non grata*. Here is the blueprint for anyone seeking success within academia in 2021. Spine not included.

All this being said, it isn't even as if these folks somehow possess arguments that are clearly and decisively better, more coherent, or more sound. Indeed, some of the more blatant contradictions and hypocrisies found on the Left warrant our explicit acknowledgement. Western science is an oppressive structure of the white-male patriarchy that we are dutybound to oppose and deconstruct, but we must trust the latest COVID-19 biomedical data. We must trust the latest

COVID-19 biomedical data, but the biomedical categories of male and female are just social constructs. The categories of male and female are just social constructs that can be chosen at will, but the category of race cannot be similarly chosen at will because race is ostensibly an objective natural kind. But race is also just a social construct. But neither of these previous claims is true since race doesn't refer to anything at all because there is only one race, the human race. But whites oppress blacks. Objective evolutionary data discredits God and objective morality, but that same evolutionary data as it relates to heritable features due to race is suddenly just a social construct again. We are in a radically relativistic, post-truth world, but we must guard against conservative fake news. There is no historical meta-narrative, but the events of slavery and colonialism are undeniable objective facts. The patriarchy of Christianity is bad, but the patriarchy of Islam, of the very same Abrahamic tradition, is to be lauded and venerated. Obesity is a social construct but also a marker of objective health at any weight. Atheist-materialist science proves that life is fundamentally meaningless and worthless, but for heaven's sake, will someone please think of the rights, dignity, and intrinsic value of animals and future generations threatened by climate change. A priori mathematics and logic are just socially constructed systems of oppression. There is no such thing as objective truth, but CNN reports just the facts. And what do we even mean by "truth" anyway? And so on. The amount of mental gymnastics required for these folks to simultaneously hold such blatant and obvious contradictions all while walking, talking, and even sometimes operating heavy machinery is truly a sight to behold, impressive as it is horrifying.

What's more, such arguments are often deployed by such folks with a self-satisfied air of condescension and a near-total lack of gratitude for anything and everything their fellow countrymen or forebears have sacrificed on their behalf, sacrifices that made the luxury of sustaining such superfluous and nonsensical arguments possible in the first place. I can honestly say now, having seen both sides, that during my time in the military I met folks who were markedly less conformist, far more open-minded, and far less vindictive towards peers and colleagues who dared to entertain or voice alternative viewpoints. My academic peers should reflect upon that last sentence carefully.

To quote Upton Sinclair, "it is difficult to get a man to understand something when his salary depends upon his not understanding it." This essay constitutes my best and most earnest attempt at communicating such understanding to my now-former colleagues. Some may call me an alarmist, a bigot, an extremist, et cetera. So be it. Such ad hominem attacks do not constitute a counterargument, nor do they do anything to take away from the one-way intersectional steamroller and one's own fixed position within the victim hierarchy. Those overly quick to dismiss what I've said here simply because I'm a straight white male should pause and take a moment to seriously reconsider their own presumed immunity from similar canceling, silencing, and cannibalization later on down the line.

That being said, I sincerely apologize to my fellow American citizens, family, friends, comrades at arms, and former colleagues for my complicity and silence on such matters for this long. No longer. It is my hope that this essay will inspire others in academia, students and professors alike, to begin speaking up loudly and vocally and to continue to speak up against this pernicious woke ideology until we bat it out the door of academia and society at large. Until then, I will continue to sound the alarm for any of those with minds and hearts open enough to hear. Listen to or dismiss these words at your own peril. However, when the woke mob comes to cancel you, when the HR department calls you into the office for mandatory remedial pronoun training, or when the agents of the pink police state come to knock at your door in the middle of the night, don't say I didn't warn you. So farewell, academia, *I disavow you.*

Dr. Michael Robillard

June 15, 2021

NOTES

Chapter One: Why Go to College?

1. *Accepted*, directed by Steve Pink (Los Angeles: Universal Pictures, 2006).

2. TalkTV, "James Delingpole: 'Universities Are Madrassas for Woke Stupidity,'" YouTube, August 8, 2020, https://www.youtube.com/watch?v=C9SWsoZRmmI.

3. William F. Buckley Jr., *God and Man at Yale* (Chicago: Regnery, 1951).

4. The Daily Wire, "Edward Feser | The Ben Shapiro Show Sunday Special Ep. 17," YouTube, September 2, 2018, https://www.youtube.com/watch?v=9FvYwpyFbIQ.

Chapter Two: Wokeism 101

1. Kenny Xu, "Harvard's Diversity Disgrace," *Spectator World*, February 2022, 38–39.

2. Ibid.

3. Kenny Xu, "A Chance for the Supremes to End Harvard's Ugly Discrimination against Asians," *New York Post*, July 4, 2021.

4. Ibid.; Xu, "Harvard's Diversity Disgrace."

5. Jacey Fortin, "Critical Race Theory: A Brief History," *New York Times*, November 8, 2021, https://www.nytimes.com/article/what -is-critical-race-theory.html.

6. Ibid.

7. The President's Advisory 1776 Commission, *The 1776 Report* (The President's Advisory 1776 Commission, 2021), https://trumpwhiteh ouse.archives.gov/wp-content/uploads/2021/01/The-Presidents-Ad visory-1776-Commission-Final-Report.pdf.

8. Robin DiAngelo, *White Fragility: Why It's So Hard for White People to Talk About Racism* (Boston: Beacon Press, 2018); Ibram X. Kendi, *How to Be an Antiracist* (New York: One World, 2019).

9. Kendi, *How to Be an Antiracist*, 9.

10. Scott Yenor, *The Recovery of Family Life: Exposing the Limits of Modern Ideologies* (Waco: Baylor University Press, 2020).

11. As of January 2022, we track all of June for "Pride Month," all of October for "LGBT History Month," and twenty-five other individual LGBT-related holidays scattered throughout the rest of the American calendar year.

12. Chadwick Moore, "This Pride, Let's Celebrate Shame," *Spectator World*, June 17, 2019, https://spectatorworld.com/topic/this-gay-pri de-lets-celebrate-shame/.

13. Hannah Bleau, "Poll: Nearly 16% of Generation Z Identify as LGBT," *Breitbart*, February 24, 2021, https://www.breitbart.com /politics/2021/02/24/poll-nearly-16-of-generation-z-identify-as-lgbt/.

14. Michael W. Chapman, "Archbishop of Krakow: Gay 'Rainbow Plague' Wants to 'Control Our Souls, Hearts and Minds,'" CNS News, August 2, 2019, https://cnsnews.com/blog/michael-w-chapman/arbp-krakow-gay-rainbow-plague-wants-control-our-souls-hearts-and-minds.

15. Carl R. Trueman, "When Evil Is Called Good," Ethics and Public Policy Center, March 3, 2022, https://eppc.org/publication/when-evil-is-called-good/.

16. Mari Mikkola, "Feminist Perspectives on Sex and Gender," *The Stanford Encyclopedia of Philosophy* (Summer 2022 edition), ed. Edward N. Zalta, https://plato.stanford.edu/entries/feminism-gender/.

17. Judith Butler, *Gender Trouble*, 10th anniversary ed. (New York: Taylor & Francis, 2002), 11.

18. "Gender and Health," World Health Organization, https://www.who.int/health-topics/gender#tab=tab_1.

19. Indeed, transgender proponents have cashed out the wrongness of "misgendering" someone in the language of disrespect, hate, wronging, harm, discrimination, threat, injustice, rights violation, human-rights violation, violence, and even erasure.

20. Rebecca Tuvel, "In Defense of Transracialism," *Hypatia* 32, no. 2 (Spring 2017): 263–78, https://doi.org/10.1111/hypa.12327.

21. Robin Dembroff and Daniel Wodak, "He/She/They/Ze," *Ergo* 5, no. 14 (2018): 371, http://dx.doi.org/10.3998/ergo.12405314.0005.014.

22. Noam Chomsky, *The Common Good* (Tuscon: Odonian Press, 1998), 43.

23. Alexander Trachtenberg, speech at the National Convention for Communist Parties in 1944 in *A Wolf in Sheep's Clothing*, directed by Stephen Payne (EWTN, 2016), https://www.imdb.com/title/tt61 07652/.

24. Sam Dorman, "Critical Race Theory–Related Ideas Found in Mandatory Programs at More than 230 Colleges, Universities: Report," Fox News, January 10, 2022, https://www.foxnews.com /us/critical-race-theory-database-colleges-universities.

25. Jonathan Butcher, "Arizona State University and Offerings at the Temple of the Woke," The Heritage Foundation, October 4, 2021, https://www.heritage.org/education/commentary/arizona-state-uni versity-and-offerings-the-temple-the-woke.

26. Jack Wolfsohn, "Decolonization: Coming to a College Near You," *National Review*, August 9, 2021, https://www.nationalreview.com /2021/08/decolonization-coming-to-a-college-near-you/.

27. Arif Ahmed, "How Our Universities Became Sheep Factories," UnHerd, January 14, 2022, https://unherd.com/2022/01/how-our -universities-became-sheep-factories/.

28. Neil Gross, "Op-Ed: Professors Are Overwhelmingly Liberal. Do Universities Need to Change Hiring Practices?," *Los Angeles Times*, May 20, 2016, https://www.latimes.com/opinion/op-ed/la-oe-gross -academia-conservatives-hiring-20160520-snap-story.html.

29. Mitchell Langbert and Sean Stevens, "Partisan Registration and Contributions of Faculty in Flagship Colleges," National Association of Scholars, January 17, 2020, https://www.nas.org/blogs/article/pa rtisan-registration-and-contributions-of-faculty-in-flagship-colleges.

30. Jon A. Shields and Joshua M. Dunn Sr., *Passing on the Right: Conservative Professors in the Progressive University* (New York: Oxford University Press, 2016).

31. Hoover Insitution, "Thomas Sowell on Intellectuals and Society," YouTube, December 16, 2009, https://www.youtube.com/watch?v=ERj3QeGw9Ok&t=451s.

32. Robert Heinlein, *Time Enough for Love: The Lives of Lazarus Long* (New York: Berkley Publishing, 1986), 137.

33. Ibid.

34. https://online.hillsdale.edu/.

35. https://www.coursera.org/.

36. https://www.angelicum.net/.

37. https://cdu.edu.

Chapter Three: The Cost of College: Why College Is Bad for Your Wallet

1. Melanie Hanson, "Average Cost of College & Tuition," EducationData.org, March 29, 2022, https://educationdata.org/average-cost-of-college; Melanie Hanson, "Average Cost of Community College," EducationData.org, December 27, 2021, https://educationdata.org/average-cost-of-community-college; Melanie Hanson, "Average Cost of Law School," EducationData.org, November 30, 2021, https://educationdata.org/average-cost-of-law-school; Melanie Hanson, "Average Cost of Medical School," EducationData.org, October 11, 2021, https://educationdata.org/average-cost-of-medical-school; Melanie Hanson, "Average Cost of a Doctorate Degree,"

EducationData.org, October 11, 2021, https://educationdata.org/av erage-cost-of-a-doctorate-degree; Melanie Hanson, "Average Cost of a Master's Degree," EducationData.org, October 11, 2021, https:// educationdata.org/average-cost-of-a-masters-degree; Melanie Hanson, "Average Cost of College Textbooks," EducationData.org, August 12, 2021, https://educationdata.org/average-cost-of-college -textbooks. These general numbers are further confirmed by "How Much Does College Cost," CollegeData.com, https://www.colleged ata.com/resources/pay-your-way/whats-the-price-tag-for-a-college -education.

2.   Hanson, "Average Cost of College & Tuition."

3.   *Borrowed Future*, directed by David DiCicco, starring Dave Ramsey, Anthony O'Neal, and John Delony (Ramsey Solutions, 2021), https:// www.imdb.com/title/tt14910836/?ref_=fn_al_tt_1.

4.   Alexandria Ocasio-Cortez, "Student Loan Cancellation Caucus Speech before Congress," December 2, 2021, U.S. House C-SPAN, https://www.c-span.org/video/?516352-4/house-approves-tempora ry-government-funding-resolution-221-212.

5.   "Current Student Loan Debt in the United States," www.collegede bt.com.

6.   *Borrowed Future.*

7.   Lyle Daly, "Average House Price by State in 2021," The Ascent, August 5, 2021, https://www.fool.com/the-ascent/research/average -house-price-state/.

8.   Turning Point USA, "AmericaFest 2021: Day 4, Session 1—Kayleigh McEnany, Rep. Madison Cawthorn & Charlie Kirk LIVE,"

YouTube, December 21, 2021, https://www.youtube.com/watch?v=Hczz2OL2oZE.

9. "College President Salary in the United States," Salary.com, https://www.salary.com/research/salary/benchmark/college-president-salary.

10. Allana Akhtar and Taylor Borden, "15 College Presidents Who've Been Paid Millionaire Salaries," Business Insider, September 15, 2020, https://www.businessinsider.com/the-highest-paid-us-college-and-university-presidents-2019-5.

11. "United States Senate Financial Disclosure Report for New Employee and Candidate Reports," Snopes.com, September 4, 2011, https://www.snopes.com/uploads/2020/01/ElizabethWarrenSenateCampaignDisclosure.pdf.

12. David Murrell, "Penn Paid Joe Biden $775,000 to Expand Its 'Global Outreach'…and Give Some Speeches," *Philadelphia*, July 10, 2019, https://www.phillymag.com/news/2019/07/10/joe-biden-penn-salary/.

13. Jeff McDonald and Morgan Cook, "Audit Launched for Cal State San Marcos Dean, Whose Expenses Feature First Class Travel, Chauffeurs and a $110 Steak," *San Diego Union-Tribune*, September 5, 2019, https://www.sandiegouniontribune.com/news/watchdog/story/2019-09-04/chauffeurs-first-class-air-and-a-110-steak-all-in-a-days-work-for-cal-state-san-marcos-dean.

14. Caroline Simon, "Bureaucrats and Buildings: The Case for Why College Is So Expensive," *Forbes*, September 5, 2017, https://www.forbes.com/sites/carolinesimon/2017/09/05/bureaucrats-and-buildings-the-case-for-why-college-is-so-expensive/?sh=11292459456a.

15. New England Center for Investigative Reporting, "New Analysis Shows Problematic Boom in Higher Ed Administrators," HuffPost, February 6, 2014, https://www.huffpost.com/entry/higher-ed-admi nistrators-growth_n_4738584.

16. Matthew D. Hendricks, "Opinion: Mills College Spent More on Administration than Instruction," *San Jose Mercury News*, February 16, 2022, https://www.mercurynews.com/2022/02/16/opinion-mil ls-college-financial-crisis-due-to-bloated-administration/.

17. "Ohio State University Spending Over $13 million a Year on Diversity Coordinators," The Palace Intrigue (Substack), December 6, 2021, https://palaceintrigueblog.com/2021/12/06/ohio-state-university-sp ending-over-13-million-a-year-on-diversity-coordinators/.

18. Robert Nozick, "Why Do Intellectuals Oppose Capitalism," Libertarianism.org, January 1, 1998, https://www.libertarianism.org /publications/essays/why-do-intellectuals-oppose-capitalism.

19. "President Barack Obama's 18 Comments on What Students Should Do after Graduating High School," Politifact, https://www.politifa ct.com/collegespeeches/.

20. President Biden (@POTUS), "12 years is no longer enough to compete...," Twitter, April 28, 2021, 7:35 p.m., https://twitter.com /POTUS/status/1387581286034939904. Similar to President Obama's remarks above.

21. https://www.goacta.org/.

22. Aaron Clarey, *Worthless: The Young Person's Indispensable Guide to Choosing the Right Major* (Excelsior, Minnesota: Paric Publishing, 2011), 27.

23. Ibid., 27–28.

24. Edwin W. Koc et al., *NACE Salary Survey* (Bethlehem, Pennsylvania: National Association of Colleges and Employers, 2019), 5.

25. Kenin M. Spivak, "The Folly of 'Woke' Math," *National Review*, September 16, 2021, https://www.nationalreview.com/2021/09/the -folly-of-woke-math/.

26. "MAT192H1: Liberating Mathematics," University of Toronto Faculty of Arts & Science, 2021, https://artsci.calendar.utoronto.ca /course/mat192h1. (This course page has been removed, but the text of the course description may be found here: https://whyevolutionis true.com/2021/11/05/the-new-math-in-toronto/.)

27. Piper Harron, "Get Out of the Way," Inclusion/Exclusion, AMS Blogs, May 11, 2017, https://blogs.ams.org/inclusionexclusion/2017 /05/11/get-out-the-way/.

28. Piper Harron, "Welcome to…Whatever This Is (Pandemic)," The Liberated Mathematician, 2015, http://www.theliberatedmathemat ician.com/.

29. Piper Harron, "The CV of a Liberated Mathematician," The Liberated Mathematician, 2015, http://www.theliberatedmathemat ician.com/cv/.

30. John Stossel, "The Woke AMA," Townhall.com, February 23, 2022, https://townhall.com/columnists/johnstossel/2022/02/23/the-woke -ama-n2603652 (ellipses in original).

31. Christine Rosen, "The Wrath of the Woke Workforce," *Commentary*, April 4, 2019, https://www.commentary.org/christine-rosen/the-wr ath-of-the-woke-workforce/.

Chapter Four: The Sciences Won't Save You: Why STEM Has Its Limits

1. Winston Churchill, "Their Finest Hour," speech in the House of Commons, International Churchill Society, June 18, 1940, https:// winstonchurchill.org/resources/speeches/1940-the-finest-hour/their -finest-hour/.

2. Paul Feyerabend, *Knowledge, Science and Relativism* (Cambridge: Cambridge University Press, 1999), 224.

3. Edward Feser, "Scientism: America's State Religion," The American Mind, August 25, 2020, https://americanmind.org/salvo/scientism -americas-state-religion/.

4. Gustaf Kilander, "'Attacks on Me Are Attacks on Science': Fauci Blasts Critics in Fiery TV Appearance," *The Independent*, June 9, 2021, https://www.independent.co.uk/news/world/americas/us-pol itics/fauci-interview-today-science-covid-b1862899.html. See also, Michael Brendan Dougherty, "Anthony Fauci: I Am the Science," *National Review*, November 29 2021, https://www.nationalreview .com/2021/11/anthony-fauci-i-am-the-science/.

5. Richard Lewontin, "Billions and Billions of Demons," *New York Review*, January 9, 1997, (reviewing the book *The Demon Haunted World: Science as a Candle in the Dark* by Carl Sagan).

6. Sarah Umer, "RETRACTED ARTICLE: A Brief History of Human Evolution: Challenging Darwin's Claim," *International Journal of Anthropology and Ethnology* 2, no. 6 (2018), https://doi.org/10.11 86/s41257-018-0014-2.

7. "The Big Bang Model is a broadly accepted theory for the origin and evolution of our universe. It postulates that 12 to 14 billion years ago, the portion of the universe we can see today was only a few

millimeters across. It has since expanded from this hot dense state into the vast and much cooler cosmos we currently inhabit. We can see remnants of this hot dense matter as the now very cold cosmic microwave background radiation which still pervades the universe and is visible to microwave detectors as a uniform glow across the entire sky." "Big Bang Cosmology," Universe 101: Big Bang Theory, NASA, March 1, 2012, https://wmap.gsfc.nasa.gov/universe/bb_th eory.html. For information on NASA, see Conservapedia, s.v. "National Aeronautics and Space Administration," September 1, 2019, https://www.conservapedia.com/National_Aeronautics_and _Space_Administration.

8. Duncan Aikman, "Lemaître Follows Two Paths to Truth," *New York Times*, February 19, 1933.

9. Mark Midbon, "'A Day without Yesterday': Georges Lemaître & the Big Bang," *Commonweal Magazine* 127, no. 6 (March 24, 2000): 18–19, https://www.catholiceducation.org/en/science/faith -and-science/a-day-without-yesterday-georges-lemaitre-amp-the-big -bang.html.

10. David Castelvecchi, "Einstein's Lost Theory Uncovered," *Nature*, February 25, 2014, https://www.scientificamerican.com/article/eins teins-lost-theory-uncovered/.

11. Ross Pomeroy, "Why Georges Lemaître Should Be as Famous as Einstein," *Live Science*, March 10, 2017, https://www.livescience .com/58204-lemaitre-should-be-famous-like-einstein.html.

12. Jerry A. Bell, *Chemistry: A Project of the American Chemical Society* (New York: W. H. Freeman, 2005), 167. For information on the American Chemical Society, see Conservopedia, s.v. "American

Chemical Society," July 13, 2016, https://www.conservapedia.com/American_Chemical_Society.

13. Neil A. Manson, *God and Design: The Teleological Argument and Modern Science* (New York: Routledge, 2003).

14. David H. Clark and Matthew D. H. Clark, *Measuring the Cosmos: How Scientists Discovered the Dimensions of the Universe* (New Brunswick: Rutgers University Press, 2004), 138.

15. "Archbishop of Canterbury Rowan Williams has flatly dismissed famed scientist Stephen Hawking's claim that gravity, not God, was responsible for creating the universe." Al Webb, "Anglican Head Rebuts Famous Scientist on God's Role in Big Bang," Good Faith Media, September 6, 2020, https://goodfaithmedia.org/anglican-head-rebuts-famous-scientist-on-god-s-role-in-big-bang-cms-16630/.

16. "However, the God of the Bible does 'new' things (Isaiah 43:19). God's creative activity was not over and done in the beginning. More is to come. Astrophysicists tell us that our universe is not eternal. It had a beginning, the big bang. It is constantly changing. New stars are born every day; while older stars morph through phases and die. The entire cosmos is expanding. It is likely that in the future the universe will wind down to a state of equilibrium and virtually die. Reality is not fixed. If we are to think of this universe as creation, we must think of it as a story, as a history, replete with change. In the dialogue between science and faith, theologians such as the late Arthur Peacocke and Robert John Russell stress continuing creation, *creatio continua.* One can hold together *creatio ex nihilo* applied to the beginning of creation's history while also holding that God's creative activity is ongoing, creatio continua." Ted Peters, "Uses and

Misuses of Creation," *Lutheran Partners Magazine* 25, no. 6 (December 2009), http://web.archive.org/web/20091108070627/ht tp://www.elca.org/Growing-In-Faith/Vocation/Lutheran-Partners /Complete-Issue/091112/091112_04.aspx.

17. "Today, the majority of physicists agree that evidence shows the universe had a beginning in an instant of a 'big bang' of energy. While Christian teaching about the Creator is not bound to any scientific theory in any age, our best scientific evidence today is consonant with Christian teaching that has been based upon revelation for two millennia." Timothy W. Whitaker, "A UM New Service Commentary by Bishop Timothy W. Whitaker: Why Should I Be a Christian?," Church and Society, August 22, 2008 https://tnc ands.blogspot.com/2008/08/um-new-service-commentary-by-bish op.html.

18. Michael Corey, *God and the New Cosmology: The Anthropic Design Argument* (Lanham: Rowman & Littlefield, 1993), 246.

19. Karen Armstrong, *The Case for God* (New York: Anchor Books, 2010), 310.

20. Robert Jastrow, "Does God Really Exist?," *Watchtower Magazine*, February 15, 1981; Robert J. Russell, *Cosmology: From Alpha to Omega; the Creative Mutual Interaction of Theology and Science* (Minneapolis: Fortress Press, 2008).

21. Helge S. Kragh, *Entropic Creation: Religious Contexts of Thermodynamics and Cosmology* (Aldershot: Ashgate, 2008), 135.

22. "It is apparent that Soviet atheism does not only deny the existence of God but expressly desires to propagate its denial of God as the

only correct atheism, the orthodox disbelief. The 'bourgeois atheism' of the West then appears as an error within atheism. In Soviet atheist literature the difference between 'bourgeois atheism' and its own 'scientific atheism' is continually stressed. Soviet atheism is also called 'the highest form of atheism' (*vysshaya stepen' ateizma*), and that is certainly the most correct assessment of Soviet atheism." William van den Bercken, "Ideology and Atheism in the Soviet Union," *Religion in Communist Lands* 13, no. 3 (1985): 281, https://mail.biblicalstudies.org.uk/pdf/rcl/13-3_269.pdf.

23. Ibid., 279.

24. Ibid., 271.

25. Kragh, *Entropic Creation*, 223.

26. I. Prokofieva, "Conference sur les questions ideologiques de l'astronomie," *La Pensee* no. 28 (1950): 12.

27. V. M. Zubok and Konstantin Pleshakov, *Inside the Kremlin's Cold War: from Stalin to Khrushchev* (Cambridge: Harvard University Press, 1996), 119.

28. Kragh, *Entropic Creation*, 224.

29. Helge Kragh, "The Universe, the Cold War, and Dialectical Materialism," arXiv, April 15, 2012, 3.

30. Ibid., 27–28.

31. Ibid., 1.

32. Ibid., 25.

33. Peter Wood, "Xi's Campus Coup," *Spectator World*, February 2022, 26–27.

34. Loren R. Graham, *Science in Russia and the Soviet Union: A Short History* (Cambridge: Cambridge University Press, 1994), 146–47.

35. Loren R. Graham, "The Socio-Political Roots of Boris Hessen: Soviet Marxism and the History of Science," *Social Studies of Science* 15, no. 4 (November 1985): 705–22.

36. Graham, *Science in Russia*, 148.

37. Ibid.

38. "Gregor Mendel (1822–1884)," DNA Learning Center, Cold Spring Harbor Laboratory, https://dnalc.cshl.edu/view/16151-Biography -1-Gregor-Mendel-1822-1884-.html.

39. *Atlas World Press Review*, vol. 24 (1977).

40. George Aiken Taylor, ed., *The Presbyterian Journal*, vol. 31 (Madison, Wisconsin: Southern Presbyterian Journal Company, 1972), https://www.google.com/books/edition/The_Presbyterian_Jo urnal/baTtAAAAMAAJ?hl=en.

41. *Australasian Journal of Psychology and Philosophy*, vol. 23–27 (Ann Arbor, Michigan: Australasian Association of Psychology and Philosophy, 1945), https://www.google.com/books/edition/The_Au stralasian_Journal_of_Psychology_a/uCsRAQAAMAAJ?hl=en&g bpv=0 .

42. "In the Soviet Union, for example, a botanist named Lysenko convinced Stalin back in the 30s that genetics was incompatible with the development of Communism. As a result, genetics was suppressed in Russia for about 25 years." James C. Hefley, *Life in the Balance* (Wheaton, Illinois: Victor Books, 1980), 76.

43. National Academy of Sciences, Committee on the Conduct of Science, National Academy of Engineering, and Institute of Medicine, *On Being A Scientist: Responsible Conduction in Research* (Washington, D.C.: National Academy Press, 2002), 7.

44. Andrew Pinsent, "New Atheists and Old Atheists," *Philosophy Now*, 2010. Pinsent even adds the ironic comparison to Lemaître: "Furthermore, as late as 1948, Soviet astronomers resolved to oppose the 'reactionary-idealistic' theory that is today called the Big Bang—first proposed by another Catholic priest, Fr Georges Lemaître. This theory of a finite widening of the universe would help 'clericalism', they warned."

45. Anna C. Pai, *Foundations of Genetics: a Science for Society* (New York: McGraw-Hill, 1974), 288.

46. Sam Kean, "The Soviet Era's Deadliest Scientist Is Regaining Popularity in Russia," *The Atlantic*, December 19, 2017, https://www.theatlantic.com/science/archive/2017/12/trofim-lysenko-soviet-union-russia/548786/.

Chapter Five: Adult Day Care: Why College Will Retard Your Maturity

1. OIED Staff, "What Is a Safe Space?," Office for Institute Equity and Diversity News, NC State University, February 7, 2020, https://diversity.ncsu.edu/news/2020/02/07/what-is-a-safe-space/. See also: TBS Staff, "What Is a Safe Space in College?," The Best Schools, March 24, 2021, https://thebestschools.org/resources/safe-space-college/. The article states: "Safe spaces are places reserved for marginalized individuals to come together and discuss their experiences. Marginalized groups may include women, people of color, survivors

of abuse, and/or members of the LGBTQIA+ community. Colleges often provide safe spaces, both on campus and online, through student groups and counseling resources. Safe spaces originated within the community now known as LGBTQIA+ and have since been adapted for use by other marginalized communities as well. Today, 'safe zones' are typically for the LGBTQIA+ community, while other marginalized communities have their own versions of safe spaces. Regardless of the name, safe spaces and safe zones are intended to facilitate communication and self-expression without fear of further marginalization."

2. Robby Soave, "UPenn Created a Post-Election Safe Space Complete with Puppies and Coloring Books," *Reason*, November 11, 2016, https://reason.com/2016/11/11/upenn-created-a-post-election-safe-space/; Robby Soave, "Elite Campuses Offer Students Coloring Books, Puppies to Get over Trump," Daily Beast, November 16, 2016, https://www.thedailybeast.com/elite-campuses-offer-students-coloring-books-puppies-to-get-over-trump.

3. SheCares Editorial Team, "Fertility and Age," SheCares, June 18, 2020, https://www.shecares.com/pregnancy/fertility/fertility-and-age.

4. Jovana Lekovich, "How Age Impacts Your Fertility," Progyny, https://progyny.com/education/age-fertility/.

5. Aristotle, *Aristotle's Politics: Writings from the Complete Works: Politics, Economics, Constitution of Athens* (Princeton University Press, 2016), 254.

6. Wikipedia, s.v. "Arrested Development," April 19, 2022, https://en.wikipedia.org/wiki/Arrested_development.

7. Katy Steinmetz, "This is What Adulting Means," *Time*, June 8, 2016, https://time.com/4361866/adulting-definition-meaning/.

8. "US Birth Rate Falls 4% to Its Lowest Point Ever," BBC News, May 6, 2021, https://www.bbc.com/news/world-us-canada-57003722.

9. Aristotle, *Nicomachean Ethics*, book 2.

10. Rebecca Traister, "Feminists Killed Home Ec. Now They Should Bring It Back—for Boys and Girls," *New Republic*, May 28, 2014, https://newrepublic.com/article/117876/feminists-should-embrace -home-economics.

11. Lynn Sherr, "What Has Been Done and What Should Be Done," *New York Times*, October 5, 1975, https://www.nytimes.com/1975 /10/05/archives/what-has-been-done-and-should-be-done-the-politi cs-of-womens.html.

12. "Modern Parenthood: Roles of Moms and Dads Converge as They Balance Work and Family," Pew Research Center, March 14, 2013, https://www.pewresearch.org/social-trends/2013/03/14/modern-pa renthood-roles-of-moms-and-dads-converge-as-they-balance-work -and-family/.

13. Betsey Stevenson and Justin Wolfers, "The Paradox of Declining Female Happiness," *American Economic Journal Economic Policy, American Economic Association* 1, no. 2 (2009): 190–225, https:// law.yale.edu/sites/default/files/documents/pdf/Intellectual_Life/Stev enson_ParadoxDecliningFemaleHappiness_Dec08.pdf.

14. Anna Petherick, "Gains in Women's Rights Haven't Made Women Happier. Why Is That?," *The Guardian*, May 18, 2016, https://www .theguardian.com/lifeandstyle/2016/may/18/womens-rights-happin ess-wellbeing-gender-gap.

15. Associated Press, "College Students Turn to 'Adulting' Classes for Basic Life Skills," Fox Business, November 18, 2019, https://www.fo xbusiness.com/money/college-students-turn-to-adulting-classes-for -basic-life-skills.

16. Elizabeth Warren and Amelia Warren Tyagi, *The Two Income Trap: Why Middle-Class Mothers and Fathers are Going Broke*, reprint ed. (New York: Basic Books, 2003).

17. Derek Thompson, "Why Child Care Is So Ridiculously Expensive," *The Atlantic*, November 26, 2019, https://www.theatlantic.com/ide as/archive/2019/11/why-child-care-so-expensive/602599/.

18. Sarah Chamberlain, "Addressing the Skilled Labor Shortage in America," *Forbes*, August 21, 2019, https://www.forbes.com/sites /sarahchamberlain/2019/08/21/addressing-the-skilled-labor-shorta ge-in-america/?sh=7dc755a181df.

19. Guy Raz, "Are People with 'Dirty Jobs' the Most Successful?," NPR, November 1, 2013, https://www.npr.org/transcripts/240780579.

20. You can find more information about trades-based schools and skills at https://www.skillsusa.org and at https://www.mikeroweworks .org.

21. Mark Antonio Wright, "*Dirty Jobs* Star Delivers Devastating Rebuke about America's Work Ethic," *National Review*, June 12, 2015, https://www.nationalreview.com/2015/06/dirty-jobs-star-delivers-de vastating-rebuke-about-americas-work-ethic-mark-antonio/.

22. Mike Rowe, "The 'Big Lesson' Mike Rowe Learned Several Hundred Times," CNN, October 18, 2014, https://edition.cnn.com/2014/10 /15/opinion/rowe-right-career/.

23. Joseph Curl, "Mike Rowe Rips Student-Loan Crisis: 'We're Rewarding Behavior We Should Be Discouraging,'" November 9, 2019, https://www.dailywire.com/news/mike-rowe-rips-student-lo an-crisis-were-rewarding-behavior-we-should-be-discouraging; "Good Magazine: America's Dirtiest Interview (Yet)," Mike Rowe, October 12, 2010, https://mikerowe.com/2010/10/good-magazine -americas-dirtiest-interview-yet/.

24. Knowland Knows, "Squats and Social Constructs," YouTube, August 18, 2021, https://www.youtube.com/watch?v=q6U8SVA I5Yg.

25. Charles D. Eden, "Harvard Sex Fair Is OK, Single-Sex Clubs, No," *Wall Street Journal*, April 24, 2016, https://www.wsj.com/articles/ha rvard-sex-fair-is-ok-single-sex-clubs-no-1461530068.

26. Travis R. Kavulla, "The Puppetry of H Bomb," *Harvard Crimson*, March 23, 2004, https://www.thecrimson.com/article/2004/3/23/ the-puppetry-of-h-bomb-rape/.

27. Justin Lehmiller, "Why the Harvard 'Munch' Club Is Not Actual News," Sex & Psychology, December 2, 2012, https://www.sexand psychology.com/blog/2012/12/2/why-the-harvard-munch-club-is -not-actual-news/; Samantha Kohl, "Squirm Carves Out Space for Exploration of Sex, Sexuality," *Miscellany News*, March 26, 2014, https://miscellanynews.org/2014/03/26/arts/squirm-carves-out-spa ce-for-exploration-of-sex-sexuality/.

28. Christy Piña, "Top 10 Colleges for Hookups," *College Magazine*, March 28, 2017, https://www.collegemagazine.com/top-10-colleges -hookups/.

29. Bob Curley, "Why Young Adults, Especially Men, Are Having Sex Less Frequently," Healthline, June 17, 2020, https://www.healthline.com/health-news/young-adults-especially-men-having-sex-less-frequently.

30. Rudyard Kipling, "The Gods of the Copybook Headings" (Garden City, New York: Doubleday, 1919).

31. Robert Shibley, "Antioch's Infamous Sexual Assault Policy," Fire, June 15, 2007, https://www.thefire.org/antiochs-infamous-sexual-assault-policy/.

32. Jake New, "The 'Yes Means Yes,' World," Inside Higher Ed, October 17, 2014, https://www.insidehighered.com/news/2014/10/17/colleges-across-country-adopting-affirmative-consent-sexual-assault-policies.

33. Alia Wong, Why the Prevalence of Campus Sexual Assault Is So Hard to Quantify," *The Atlantic*, January 26, 2016, https://www.theatlantic.com/education/archive/2016/01/why-the-prevalence-of-campus-sexual-assault-is-so-hard-to-quantify/427002/.

34. J. D. Unwin, *Sex and Culture* (London: Oxford University Press, 1934).

35. John Glubb, *The Fate of Empires and Search for Survival* (Edinburgh: William Blackwood & Sons, 1977), 15, http://people.uncw.edu/kozloffm/glubb.pdf.

Chapter Six: What a University Should Be (and Where It's Going)

1. Karl Marx, *Theses on Feuerbach* (1845), thesis 11.

2. New World Encyclopedia, s.v. "Thomism," https://www.newworldencyclopedia.org/entry/Thomism.

3. *Encyclopedia Britannica Online*, s.v. "Natural Law," https://www
.britannica.com/topic/natural-law.

4. Ibid.

5. See appendix for the rest of the farewell essay.

6. Julian Huxley, *New Bottles for New Wine* (New York: Harper,
1957), 17.

7. Nick Bostrom, "Human Genetic Enhancements: A Transhumanist
Perspective," *Journal of Value Inquiry* 37, no. 4 (December 2003):
493–506, https://www.nickbostrom.com/ethics/genetic.html.

8. Ray Kurzweil, "The Laws of Accelerating Returns," Kurzweil,
March 7, 2001, https://www.kurzweilai.net/the-law-of-accelerating
-returns.

9. Robert Wiblin, Arden Koehler, and Keiran Harris, "Toby Ord on
the Precipice and Humanity's Potential Futures," 80,000 Hours,
March 7, 2020, https://80000hours.org/podcast/episodes/toby-ord
-the-precipice-existential-risk-future-humanity/.

10. Aria Bendix, "An Oxford Philosopher Who's Inspired Elon Musk
Thinks Mass Surveillance Might Be the Only Way to Save Humanity
from Doom," Business Insider Nederland, April 19, 2019 (emphasis
added).

11. H. G. Wells, *The Open Conspiracy: Blue Prints for a World
Revolution* (London: Gollancz, 1933; Project Gutenberg, 2013),
chapters 7–8, 14, 18.

Chapter Seven: How to Teach Yourself Philosophy (and Do the Same for Other Subjects)

1. Quoted in Joseph M. Holden, *The Comprehensive Guide to Apologetics* (Eugene, Oregan: Harvest House Publishers, 2022), 381.

2. Will Durant, *The Story of Philosophy* (New York: Washington Square Press, 1961), xxvi–xxvii.

3. "Plato; Or, the Philosopher," Ralph Waldo Emerson (1803–1882), https://emersoncentral.com/texts/representative-men/plato-or-the-philosopher/.

4. Alfred North Whitehead, *Process and Reality* (New York; Free Press, 2010), 39.

5. Quoted in Durant, *Story of Philosophy*, footnote, 59.

6. Thomas Aquinas, *Aquinas's Shorter Summa: Saint Thomas's Own Concise Version of His Summa Theologica* (Nashua, New Hampshire: Sophia Institute Press, 2001); Thomas Aquinas, *Thomas Aquinas: Selected Writings*, ed. Ralph McInerny (New York: Penguin Classics, 1999); Thomas Aquinas, *The Aquinas Catechism: A Simple Explanation of the Catholic Faith by the Church's Greatest Theologian* (Nashua, New Hampshire: Sophia Institute Press, 2000); Thomas Aquinas, *A Summa of the Summa*, ed. Peter Kreeft (San Francisco: Ignatius Press, 1990).

7. New World Encyclopedia, s.v. "Thomism," https://www.newworldencyclopedia.org/entry/Thomism.

8. Friedrich Nietzsche, *The Pre-Platonic Philosophers* (Urbana, Illinois: University of Illinois Press, 2001), 3.

9. Parmenides hailed from Elea and believed that all of existence was one, unified, static being. As noted above, he maintained that change was specious and merely apparent. Indeed, how could change and motion truly be affirmed when unchanging principles of the universe (e.g., the definition of triangularity) admit of no change or motion whatsoever? Accordingly, students of Parmenides such as Zeno composed "proofs" of the ostensible duplicity of change.

10. Nietzsche, *Pre-Platonic Philosophers*, 80–81.

11. Heraclitus hailed from Ephesus and believed that all of existence was Becoming: meaningless, changing, diverse flux.

12. Madsen Pirie, "Heraclitus v. Paremenides—Flux v. Stasis," Adam Smith Institute, July 20, 2015, https://www.adamsmith.org/blog/philosophy/heraclitus-v-parmenides-flux-v-stasis.

13. Nietzsche, *Pre-Platonic Philosophers*, 62.

14. Pirie, "Heraclitus v. Parmenides."

15. New World Encyclopedia, s.v. "Form and Matter," https://www.newworldencyclopedia.org/entry/Form_and_Matter.

16. Edward Feser, "Four Causes and Five Ways," Blogger.com, June 6, 2016, http://edwardfeser.blogspot.com/2016/06/four-causes-and-five-ways.html.

17. Aristotle, *Metaphysics*, book 12, section 1073a14–15.

18. Francis Bacon used this moniker for his great reformation of human knowledge in the work of the same title *Instauratio Magna*.

19. Pope Benedict XVI, "The Regensburg Address," September 12, 2006.

20. Pedro Cintas, "Francis Bacon: An Alchemical Odyssey through the *Novum Organum*," *Bulletin for the History of Chemistry* 28, no. 2 (2003): 66.

21. *Encyclopedia Britanica Online*, s.v. "alchemy," https://www.britan nica.com/topic/alchemy.

22. Fabrizio Bigotti, "Corpuscularianism," in *Encyclopedia of Early Modern Philosophy and the Sciences*, ed. Dana Jalobeanu and Charles T. Wolfe (Cham, Switzerland: Springer International Publishing, 2020), 1–13, https://doi.org/10.1007/978-3-319-20791-9_133-1.

23. Cintas, "Francis Bacon," 65–66.

24. Internet Encyclopedia of Philosophy, s.v ,"René Descartes (1596–1650)," by Justin Skirry, https://iep.utm.edu/rene-descartes/.

25. Karen Detlefsen, "Teleology and Natures in Descartes' Sixth Meditation," in *Descartes' Meditations: A Critical Guide* (Cambridge: Cambridge University Press, 2013), 153–76.

26. Encyclopedia.com, s.v. "Philosophy of Science: Baconian and Cartesian Approaches," by Lois N. Magner, https://www.encyclop edia.com/science/encyclopedias-almanacs-transcripts-and-maps/ph ilosophy-science-baconian-and-cartesian-approaches.

27. Darwin's explicit Deism seemed to do little to stand against this greater materialist picture.

28. Roger Kiska, "Antonio Gramsci's Long March through History," *Acton Institute* 29, no. 3 (December 12, 2019), https://www.acton .org/religion-liberty/volume-29-number-3/antonio-gramscis-long-ma rch-through-history.

Chapter Eight: Double-Agentry: How to Subvert the Radicals (If You Must Go to College)

1. Walt Whitman, "Oh Me! Oh Life!," in *Leaves of Grass* (1892).

2. Santi Ruiz, "Microsoft Encourages Employees to State Race, Gender during Presentations," Washington Free Beacon, November 8, 2021, https://freebeacon.com/culture/microsoft-encourages-employees-to -state-race-gender-during-presentations/.

3. David Garrow, "The Troubling Legacy of Martin Luther King," *Standpoint*, June 2019, https://www.davidgarrow.com/wp-content /uploads/2019/05/DJGStandpoint2019.pdf.

4. Ibid. The book for which Garrow won the Pulitzer Prize is titled *Bearing the Cross: Martin Luther King, Jr., and the Southern Christian Leadership Conference* (New York: William Morrow, 1986).

5. Ibid.

6. For an in-depth and excellent fine-grained account of these kinds of tactics and tactics like them, see the book *Counter Wokecraft: A Field Manual for Combatting the Woke in University and Beyond* (Independently published, 2021) by Charles Pincourt and James Lindsay. Also see Saul Alinksy's left-wing classic *Rules for Radicals* (New York: Vintage Books, 1971) as well as Timothy and David Gordon's *Rules for Retrogrades* (Charlotte, North Carolina: TAN Books, 2020) for other helpful conceptual frameworks and tactics in this same vein.

7. Dinesh D'Souza, "How the West Grew Rich," *Washington Times*, June 16, 2003, https://www.washingtontimes.com/news/2003/jun /16/20030616-093350-3933r/.

8. Aleksandr Solzhenitsyn, "Live Not by Lies," The Aleksandr Solzhenitsyn Center, February 12, 1974, https://www.solzhenitsync enter.org/live-not-by-lies.

Conclusion: The Evil of the Ivory Tower

1. Fox News, "'Campus Craziness': College Stops Flying American Flag," YouTube, November 21, 2016, https://www.youtube.com/wa tch?v=HQD5BvU6SI4.

2. Stanley Kurtz, "The Campus Free-Speech Crisis Deepens," *National Review*, September 27, 2017, https://www.nationalreview.com/corn er/campus-free-speech-crisis-deepens/.

3. "Reed College Bows to the Bullies," (editorial), *Wall Street Journal*, April 20, 2018, https://www.wsj.com/articles/reed-college-bows-to -the-bullies-1524179901.

4. Amber Athey, "UNO Provides Glossary of 'Queer and Trans Community' Terms," Campus Reform, March 15, 2017, https:// www.campusreform.org/?ID=8929.

5. Anthony Gockowski, "'PC Madness Bracket' Ranks Campus Craziness," Campus Reform, March 16, 2017, https://www.campu sreform.org/?ID=8932.

6. Itay Hod, "Middlebury Professor Speaks Out about Mob That 'Gave Me a Concussion,'" The Wrap, March 13, 2017, https://www.thew rap.com/middlebury-professor-speaks-mob-gave-concussion/.

7. Bret Weinstein (@BretWeinstein), "Credible reports protestors w/bats roaming campus...," Twitter, June 5, 2017, 5:00 p.m., https://twit ter.com/bretweinstein/status/8718643216298680033?lang=en; Nick

Roll, "Evergreen Professor Receives $500,000 Settlement," Inside Higher Ed, September 18, 2017, https://www.insidehighered.com/qu icktakes/2017/09/18/evergreen-professor-receives-500000-settlement.

8. George Ciccariello (@ciccmaher), "All I Want for Christmas is White Genocide," Twitter, December 24, 2016, 7:48 p.m., https://twitter .com/ciccmaher/status/812867490002927616. Thought the tweet has been removed, a screenshot is located at https://archive.ph /rpWK8.

9. Gockowski, "'PC Madness Bracket.'"

10. Ibid.

11. Ibid.

12. Emilie Raguso, "Eric Clanton Takes 3-Year Probation Deal in Berkeley Rally Bike Lock Assault Case," Berkeleyside, August 8, 2018, https://www.berkeleyside.org/2018/08/08/eric-clanton-takes -3-year-probation-deal-in-berkeley-rally-bike-lock-assault-case.

13. Dorothy Cummings McLean, "'Absolutely Surreal': Student Mob Smashes Window in Protest against Jordan Peterson," LifeSiteNews, March 6, 2018, https://www.lifesitenews.com/news/absolutely-surr eal-student-mob-smashes-window-in-protest-against-jordan-pet/.

14. Hayden Williams, "I Was Assaulted at Berkeley Because I'm Conservative. Free Speech Is under Attack," *USA TODAY*, March 6, 2019, https://www.usatoday.com/story/opinion/voices/2019/03/06 /berkeley-conservative-students-campus-college-bias-punch-column /3065895002/.

15. Mary Kaye Linge, "Conservative Speaker Michael Knowles Attacked by Protester at Missouri College Campus," *New York Post*, April

13, 2019, https://nypost.com/2019/04/13/conservative-speaker-mic
hael-knowles-attacked-by-protester-at-missouri-college-campus/.

16. Josh Hafner, "'Angry White Male Studies': College's Course Draws
    Criticism from White Congressman," *USA TODAY*, April 4, 2019,
    https://www.usatoday.com/story/news/education/2019/04/04/angry
    -white-male-studies-ku-college-course-criticized-congressman/336
    8437002/.

17. Steve MacDonald, "University in Maine Asks 'Community' to Sign
    'BLM Antiracism Pledge' (So They Can Make a List of Who Did
    Not)," Granite Grok, August 8, 2020, https://granitegrok.com/blog
    /2020/08/university-in-maine-asks-community-to-sign-blm-antirac
    ism-pledge-so-they-can-make-a-list-of-who-did-not.

18. Harry Lambert, "Kathleen Stock and Sussex University: The War
    over Academic Freedom," *New Statesman*, October 20, 2021,
    https://www.newstatesman.com/politics/feminism/2021/10/kathle
    en-stock-and-sussex-university-the-war-over-academic-freedom.

19. "Gender Studies and Sexualised Threats," Sex Matters, July 26,
    2021, https://sex-matters.org/posts/updates/gender-studies-and-sex
    ualised-threats/.

20. Kenneth Garger, "UPenn Transgender Swimmer Continues
    Dominant Season with More Record-Breaking Wins," *New York
    Post*, December 7, 2021, https://nypost.com/2021/12/07/upenn-tra
    nsgender-swimmer-lia-thomas-continues-dominant-season-with-mo
    re-record-breaking-wins/.

21. Jackie Salo, "'We Got to Take These Motherf-ckers Out': Rutgers
    Professor Calls White People Villains'," *New York Post*, October 29,

2021, https://nypost.com/2021/10/29/rutgers-professor-calls-white-people-villains/.

22. Cristina Laila, "Former UCLA 'Philosophy of Race' Lecturer Arrested for Threatening to Commit Mass Shooting against White Members of Philosophy Department," Gateway Pundit, February 1, 2022, https://www.thegatewaypundit.com/2022/02/former-ucla-philosophy-race-lecturer-arrested-threatening-commit-mass-shooting-white-members-philosophy-department/.

INDEX